A Pixel in a Greater Picture

A Pixel in a Greater Picture

The Emerging Church of Christ

Fred Peatross

Foreword by Edward Fudge

Fast Forward Press

A Pixel in a Greater Picture
The Emerging Church of Christ

Copyright © 2001 by Richard Fred Peatross

All rights reserved under International and Pan-American Conventions.

This book may not be reproduced or distributed in whole or in part or electronic form including photocopied or audiotape means and methods without the written permission of the author.

Published in the United States by IndyPublish.com for Fast Forward Press.
1487 Chain Bridge Road
Suite 304
McLean, VA 22101

ISBN 1-58827-049-1
ISBN 1-58827-027-0 (Paperback)

Library of Congress Control Number: 2001088286

Dedication

To my spiritual family, The Norway Avenue Church of Christ, whose forward thinking elders are committed to making the body of Christ culturally relevant to the next generation of believers. It truly is a church for the next generation.

To my ever-patient wife who willingly became a "writer's widow."

To Dr. Tim Robarts who believed in me and encouraged me.

To Jeff Stevenson who helped me understand grace.

To my Great Commission partner and genuine friend, Michael McElroy.

To Jesse and Debbie Perry, servants of God in a time of need. Thanks!

And to the One who started me on this eternal journey, my Savior Jesus.

Epigraph

We live in a time when the church has a great opportunity to be the answer to the postmodern question. To be this answer, we must understand how the postmodern culture thinks, what it values, and how God will be received. If we continue to cling to modernism, we may miss a great opportunity for evangelism.

Contents

Foreword *by Edward Fudge*	*i*
Preface	*iii*
Acknowledgements	*v*
Introduction	*vi*
Restoration Run Amuck *by guest writer Bill Chance*	1
Beyond Tradition and Contemporary Worship	10
Diversity is Biblical	14
History Primer 101	16
Star Trek Primer 101	17
Forty-four Reasons Churches of Christ Don't Change	22
Change-agent Development	24
Nine Tips for Change Agents	26
Implementing Change	28
Baby Dedications	31
Prohibition Theology	34
Worship and Emotions	37
The World Waits	41
Even Superman Had Problems	45
The Wilderness	47
Anatomy of a Cardboard Life	50
Jesus the Scorekeeper	52
You Can't Understand	56
Musings on Human Tragedies	60
Trust	63
The Truth About Us	65
Parable of a Lobster	67
Fear, Doubt, and an Empty Tomb	69
God's Others—Thems and Theys	72
Extremophiles	73
Death Before Resurrection	78
Welcome to the X-treme Church	82
Reformation Through Team Ministry	84
Building Community	88
God So Loved the World; Why Can't the Church?	95
An Uncommon Vision	97
Engaging the World Through the Senses	99
A First Century Postmodernist	103
Present/Future Leaders	108
New Maps for a New World	111

Let's Call Her What We Want Her to Be, a Minister *by guest writer Shelley Neilson*	114
Finality	118
Conclusion	120
Epilogue	122

Foreword

Perhaps the older we get, the less we enjoy change; however, "old" is not necessarily a matter of years. I celebrated my fifty-sixth birthday this millennium year, but I have long loved the comfortable routines of life – rising at the same hour, eating the same breakfast, taking the familiar route to work. My wife reminds me occasionally that I have worn the same bow tie the last several Sundays and that it is time to change. I am sympathetic to those who prefer the familiar!

Yet the right kind of change is a necessity for a Christian. "Conversion" means changing. "Repentance" means changing. "Sanctification" means changing. "Growing" means changing. The question is not whether we change, but how and why. Churches, too, must change if they are alive and growing. Much has been written recently about change and the so-called "change agents" who promote it. Fred Peatross is definitely a "change agent," but so, he reminds us, was Jesus Christ. What I appreciate about this book is Fred's thoughtful balance between change and constancy. Some things remain the same, and he knows that. The gospel, for example. Christian living, for another. But styles change -- forms, customs, methods, structures.

Fred was not "brought up," as they say, "in the church." As an adult convert to Christ, he looks at church with fresh eyes. He does not have to overcome, as many of us do, years of familiar gazing (or is it glazing?). He is like the little boy who observed the Emperor and blurted out that the Emperor was naked. We need to hear such fresh viewpoints from people who see matters clearly.

This book is Bible-based, centered on Christ, and brimming with evangelistic zeal to bring others to know him as Savior and Lord. To accomplish that goal, nothing less important ought to get in the way. Fred helps us analyze what really matters and what does not. He gives practical tips for implementing constructive change in our churches. He writes with one eye on the contemporary culture and the other in the Scriptures. I commend what he says here for your careful consideration. Whether you agree with all or not, you will be better for having read it and letting it percolate in your mind and heart. I hope you will do just that.

–Edward Fudge

Author of the books ***The Fire That Consumes*** *and* ***Beyond The Sacred Pages.***

Edward Fudge earned B.A. and M.A. degrees in biblical languages from Abilene Christian University, studied at Covenant Theological Seminary and Eden Theological Seminary, and earned a doctorate in Jurisprudence from the University of Houston Law Center.

Preface

You and I happen to be living on the "edge" of a time in history of high "tectonic activity"—the end of one age and the beginning of another. It's a time of shaking. Yesterday's maps are already outdated, and today's soon will be, too. The uncharted world ahead of us is what we will call "the new world on the other side": the other side of two world wars and one cold war, the other side of communism, the other side of the second millennium, the other side of modernism. There used to be an Old World, then a New World, then the Third World, but now all three are being swept up in a new world.

During the last hundred years, and especially the last fifty, old-world technology has intensified cultural pressures and unleashed tremor after tremor, each far more significant than could ever before been imagined. These technological tremors have helped bring to an end the old world that created them. Think of the automobile and its effects on the environment, the economy, the family unit, and even courtship, and sexuality. Think of radio, air travel, birth-control pills, antibiotics, and the cathode ray tube, and we're barely past the mid-century mark. Then came the tidal wave of social change set in motion during the sixties. No wonder the old maps don't fit the new world!

In the church of the third millennium, the future theology will be creative pursuit and passionate inquiry, like the best art and the best science. Psychology, sociology, the new physics, history, comparative religion, and spirituality—not to mention postmodernism in general—all are calling for creative Christians to unfold new paradigms to use in new world explorations. The old systems feel tired, used up, old hat, and worn, but the thirst for God is as strong as ever. New theological wineskins? I think so.

It is my prayer that churches will begin speaking in the "heart language" of this new world and begin to create an environment where Christians are encouraged to become creative thinkers, pursuers of truth, explorers, and learners, rather than old world memorizers, repeaters, and defenders of old formulations. What a challenge we encounter when we open ourselves to discover how Jesus Christ wants to theologically incarnate himself for the postmodern world, just as he did for the post-Enlightenment world of the old church.

Read on!

Acknowledgements

My name is listed as the author of this book, but Sylvia Carey, of Shreveport, Louisiana, fine-tuned my ideas and put them into a readable form. Thank you Sylvia for your long, patient hours of meticulous editing. My appreciation for you is difficult to express with the ink of a pen.

Thank you Stuart Smith, of N.E. Lincolnshire, England, for the cover's artwork.

A special thank you to Bill Chance and Shelley Neilson for allowing a few of your thoughts to be included in the pages of this book.

As time has passed I may have forgotten where some of the ideas in this book came from. Any borrowed material has become so much a part of my belief system that I may well be mistaking it for my own. So thank you to all who may have unknowingly contributed.

Introduction

Calvin Klein's fragrance *"be"* has tapped into the social acceptance of androgyny; *"be"* is for both men and women. Obviously, what it means to be a man or a woman is no longer as clear as it used to be. Homosexuality and bisexuality have become more acceptable and mainstream; women have entered the work force yet have had to function predominantly under male rules; men are now staying at home to raise the children. With many people wondering what it means to be a man or a woman, indistinguishability has become the norm. Men can explore the female realm, and women can explore the male world. Klein uses these social changes to get his cash register ringing.

Klein has also pulled together different elements that are prevalent among the so-called "Generation X." *"Be"* says that life is lived in the moment, the now. Dr. Martin Robinson in his book *The Faith of the Unbeliever* refers to this as the perpetual present: "The voice of this generation says: 'Life can sometimes get complicated with tomorrow or yesterday. Don't ask for commitment because commitment involves more than now. Don't tell me what I must do, just let me float from one possibility to the next. I am me and that's all I can be." Or as Bart Simpson says, "I do what I *feel* like." Whereas Nike says, "Just do it." Klein says, "Just *be;*" go with the flow and let the moment dictate.

To reach and motivate this generation of people is a struggle the church will face for some time. As always we need to work *in* people, not at them. Lurking beneath their complacency are hopes, desires, and dreams. We all have yearnings in this life. If the church of the new millennium is going to communicate with people living in the *now*, she must appeal to their passions, the things that make them come alive. Only when we discover and identify what drives this generation will we begin opening up avenues of communication. It's called sharing the Gospel on someone else's terms rather than on our own.

I'm convinced that a truly effective Christian communicator is one who has a deep understanding of biblical principles, a clear grasp of contemporary culture, and the ability to analyze both and apply the one to the other. This book is an attempt to do that.

–Fred Peatross

Chapter 1
Restoration Run Amuck

William T. Chance

It was a noble idea indeed, an idea that must have had God's enthusiastic support and blessing. After all, had not God himself insisted on the purity of his people? No intermarrying, no mixing of families, no dilution of the faith. Yet that is exactly what had happened with all of those Grecian influences. They were diluting the purity of the law. They were introducing strange customs and new gods. Soon there would be no Jewish religion, culture, or nation. It would all be an amalgam, a heterogeneous group worshiping who knows what. Something had to be done to save this people for God. But who had the authority? Who had the strength? Who had the purity? So was born the Pharisee, that protector of Jewish purity, that perfect child of God who knew everyone else should be as perfect as he was, yet who also knew that no one else could achieve such perfection. That self-appointed savior of the Jewish law and father of the traditions was imposed on the masses. It was he who would restore the Jewish laws and traditions to the rightful state of purity and truth so desired by God.

The evolution of the Pharisee sect of the Jews occurred during the second century B.C. This time period was after Alexander the Great had conquered Israel. He was quite considerate to the Jewish inhabitants of his newly acquired Palestine. They were allowed to continue practicing their religion; he even offered rewards to those who agreed to resettle in Alexandria. Alexander's planting of Grecian cities throughout his conquered lands insured the rapid spread of Greek culture to those areas. Israel was not spared these Grecian influences, with inroads being made into culture, commerce, and religion. It was this contaminating situation that produced the Pharisees. They saw that there was a strong tendency among the Jews to accept Grecian culture and its pagan religious practices. The purposes of the Pharisees were to preserve the national integrity of Israel and to insure strict conformity to the Law of Moses. Thus, they sought to restore Israel to its pure state of existence, eliminating all influences of the Grecian culture or any other culture. This action, they thought, was what God himself would do if he were on earth, preserve a people unto himself who were pure, holy, and righteous, while excluding the pagan, the sinner, and the commoner.

To characterize the Pharisees as bad people is to totally misunderstand them. Indeed, they were the most righteous people of their day. They were dedicated to the Law and to doing what the Law said to do. They were lovers of the Torah and protectors of the Bible as the Word of God.

Thus, they were dogmatic about preserving the original meaning of the Scriptures. This obsession caused them to develop the oral traditions, which they believed pointed out what God really intended to say in the Bible. Consequently, they found it necessary to explain and amplify God's commandments in order to make them fit each activity of life. Their primary concern in life was to make the Torah their supreme guide. So great was their concern for not breaking the Law that they built fences around the Law, serving as warning signals to control behavior before a commandment was broken. Thus, as summarized by George Knight,[i] they developed 1,521 oral traditions (rules) for observing the Sabbath day alone. Needless to say, many more of these fences and their oral traditions existed for protecting the other commandments and controlling nearly all activities of daily living. The Pharisees were also devout tithers, and they had great missionary zeal, by which they hoped to build up the holy community of Israel. They also looked forward to the coming of the Messiah and the establishment of his kingdom. The Pharisees separated themselves from the rest of the Jews, the heathen, and the commoner. They sought to pave the way for the Christ through keeping the Law perfectly. What then was the problem with this group of holy people that led Jesus to say, *"Unless your righteousness exceeds that of the scribes and Pharisees, you will never enter the kingdom of heaven?"* (Matthew 5:20).

One answer to this question is given by Paul in Romans 9:30-32, *"What then shall we say? That the Gentiles, who did not pursue righteousness, have obtained it, a righteousness that is by faith; but Israel, who pursued a law of righteousness, has not obtained it. Why not? Because they pursued it not by faith but as if it were by works. They stumbled over the 'stumbling stone.'"* Thus, in their pursuit to get it perfect, the Pharisees had completely missed what God really wanted from them. They had totally substituted form and ritual for spirit. Their idea of righteousness had become one of keeping the law perfectly in order to please God. Thus, the righteousness that was produced was self-righteousness.

Jesus gave God's perspective on the Pharisees in Matthew 15:8, *"These people honor me with their lips, but their hearts are far from me. They worship me in vain; their teachings are but rules taught by men."* He elaborated on their problem, quoting from the prophet Isaiah, *"For this people's heart has become calloused; they hardly hear with their ears, and they have closed their eyes. Otherwise they might see with their eyes, hear with their ears, understand with their hearts and turn, and I would heal them"* (Matthew 13:15). Truly, as concluded by Luke (7:30), the Pharisees had rejected God's purpose for themselves. They had become so entrenched in restoring and preserving the Law and the distinctiveness of Israel that they had forgotten the purpose of the Law: to change peoples' hearts allowing them to become more like God. Indeed, they had ignored this fact in spite of the numerous admonitions given throughout the prophets. Thus, God said through Isaiah, *"The multitude of your sacrifices— what are they to me? I have more than enough of burnt offerings, of rams and the fat of fattened animals; I have no pleasure in the blood of bulls and lambs and goats. When you spread out your hands in prayer, I will hide my eyes from you; even if you offer many prayers, I will not listen. Your hands are full of blood; wash and make yourselves clean. Take your evil deeds out of my sight! Stop doing wrong, learn to do right! Seek justice, encourage the oppressed. Defend the cause of the fatherless, plead the case of the widow"* (1: 11,15-17). Hosea reflects a similar sentiment, *"For I desire mercy, not sacrifice, and acknowledgment of God rather than burnt offerings"* (Hosea 6: 6). Through Amos, God adds more rebukes, *"I hate, I despise your religious feasts; I cannot stand your assemblies. Even though you bring me burnt offerings and grain offerings, I will not accept them. Though you bring choice fellowship offerings, I will have no regard for them. Away with the noise of your songs! I will not listen to the music of your harps. But let justice roll on like a river, righteousness like a never-failing stream!"* (Amos 5: 21-24). Micah also relays what God has always wanted from man, *"He has showed you, O man, what is good. And what does the Lord require of you? To act justly and to love mercy and to walk humbly with your God"* (Micah 6: 8). The above passages all indicate that doing the right rituals, saying the right words, even restoring and preserving the original form are of no value to God if one's heart is not changed to become God-like. The Jews had substituted religious activity for changed hearts, and the Pharisees had become experts in this endeavor. As a result they failed to recognize God, even when he was among them. Even worse, they plotted to crucify him because his message was so different from what they believed to be the correct service to him.

In the early nineteenth century several men began reading the Word of God closely and recognized that throughout the centuries many changes had been made to doctrine, form, and ritual. Going beyond the reforming activities of Martin Luther centuries earlier, these men called for a return to the pattern of God's church as revealed in the New Testament. Their call was inclusive in nature, calling for all to leave men's traditions and embrace simple New Testament Christianity. Indeed, they were calling for a restoration of God's church as it existed originally and as they believed it was intended to exist throughout the ages.

The success of the early restorationists was impressive, with the group growing from about 20,000 when its originators, Alexander Campbell and Barton Stone, merged their groups in 1832, to nearly 200,000 in 1860. However, as summarized by Russel Paden,[ii] the unity of the movement began to exhibit signs of fragmentation as early as the 1840s, with some members being more concerned with denouncing denominational errors than with preaching the gospel. Barton Stone expressed concerns over this exclusivity saying, "Some among ourselves were for some time zealously engaged to do away with party creeds and are yet zealously preaching against them—but instead of a written creed of man's device, they have substituted a nondescript one, and exclude good brethren from their fellowship because they dare believe differently from their opinions."[iii] Alexander Campbell echoed Stone's fears saying, "Some of our brethren were too much addicted to denouncing the sects and representing them en masse as wholly aliens from salvation—as wholly antichristian and corrupt. These very zealous brethren gave countenance to the popular clamor that we make baptism a savior, or a passport to heaven, disparaging all the private and social virtues of the professing public."[iv] Thus, the founders of the restoration movement foresaw potential problems developing, with an emphasis being placed on form and function rather than on a spirit of inclusiveness.

Second generation restoration leaders, such as David Lipscomb and Austin McGary, began publishing Christian journals in which they expanded upon what was considered to be basic fundamental Christian doctrine. This expansion elaborated upon what the Christian church could and could not do and still be recognized as God's body. Their tests of potentially unacceptable activities for a church was much more restrictive than were those of their predecessors and included missionary societies, instrumental music, open communion, dancing, theater, locally paid preachers, Sunday schools, baptisteries in church buildings, and eating in church buildings. Toward the end of the nineteenth century, there existed a feeling that the restoration was complete, with primitive New Testament Christianity now existing again in its purest form. Thus, the emphasis of the restoration was no longer one of unity but exclusivity, focusing upon duplicating the patterns, methodologies, and beliefs of the first century church as closely as possible. Therefore, if one deviated from this supposedly divine pattern, even in one point, he or she would surely be displeasing to God.

This growing sense of exclusiveness lead to an official division of the restoration groups early in the twentieth century, with the southern more exclusive group becoming the Churches of Christ and the northern more inclusive group evolving into the Disciples of Christ/Christian Churches. Even after this split, however, the Churches of Christ continued to be embroiled in conflict over both old and new issues. For some leaders within the group, the near canonization of Campbell's slogan, "where the Scriptures speak, we speak, where they are silent we are silent," led to prohibition of nearly every act or institution that could not be authorized specifically in the Bible.[v] Thus, congregational cooperation, method of evangelism, missionary work, support of radio or TV programs, support of orphans' homes, widows' homes, Christian colleges, number of communion cups, eating in the church building, kitchen in churches, style of worship, with whom to fellowship, campus ministries, millennial doctrine, and various preachers' personalities have all been points of contention, resulting in divisions in the Churches of Christ.

In conceptualizing this factionalism of the Churches of Christ, Carl Etter labeled it incidentalism, saying, "The smallest incidentals in the daily experience of New Testament character was magnified into a matter of great importance and an article of faith."[vi] During the twentieth century this attitude caused many divisions within the Churches of Christ, with each faction not having fellowship or recognizing the other factions. As noted by Michael Weed, the Churches of Christ have no mechanism for resolving doctrinal controversies or deciding what is opinion and what is of faith. Although the independence of each congregation appears to have been part of God's plan for dealing with these issues, the Churches of Christ have routinely voided this mechanism by practicing congregational withdrawal of fellowship from other congregations with which they disagreed. The scriptures concerning arguments over matters of opinion (Romans 14; I Corinthians 8 and 10) also have been of little use in settling controversies since each faction typically believes that its opinion is doctrine. In a similar vein, scriptures concerning love and self-sacrifice have been ignored, with presumed doctrinal correctness taking precedence over brotherly relationships.[vii]

Thus, as summarized by Paden, the Churches of Christ view doctrinal correctness and the perfect restoration of the apostolic church on even the smallest matters as of supreme importance.[viii] Therefore, one's Christian identity and salvation came to rest on being correct in all doctrinal matters. With such a view and no clear-cut method to settle differences in biblical interpretation, the Churches of Christ could scarcely avoid continued division over seemingly trivial issues. Along with these problems, the Churches of Christ developed a very rigid unwritten creed, while decrying the creeds of denominations. This unwritten creed is centered around an attitude of exclusiveness, a sense of "historylessness," an intellectual approach to the Bible, baptism, and avoidance of instrumental music. Even the language employed by the Churches of Christ reveals the unwritten creed, by referring to the "fellowship of believers, the body of Christ, the brotherhood" in an exclusive sense, implying that all who are not like us and do not believe exactly like us are not included as referents of these words. That terminology reflects the attitude in many Churches of Christ that "we are the one true church universal," and reinforces a sense of "historylessness" in that the first century church has now been restored and "we are it." Thus, the over 1500-year gap between the pre-apostasy original and restored Church of Christ is seen as a time when God's true church did not exist upon the earth.

Therefore, this exclusive group of modern restorationists appear to have fallen into the same trap as did the Pharisees two millennia prior. They have come to rely on doctrinal purity, form, and ritual as a means of achieving and maintaining a correct relationship with God. In a very real sense, "head knowledge" has been substituted for a spiritual relationship with God. Thus, members of the Churches of Christ often have much Bible knowledge with little understanding of its spiritual meaning for their lives. In attempts at obtaining doctrinal correctness and order in worship, the Spirit has been neglected, quenched, and asked to remain outside of the building. Unfortunately, in many situations, the Spirit has also been left outside of lives, leaving worshippers with a cold, but orderly worship, which allows few to appreciate the majesty of God.

Congregations of the Churches of Christ exist as independent local bodies, complete with their own group of overseers; therefore, great diversity may be found among the various churches. Some congregations may openly embrace the Spirit of the Lord and not be afraid of the Spirit's manifestation. Many other Churches of Christ, however, are restrictive and exclusive in their philosophy. These churches prohibit all activities not identified in their unwritten creed. This focus upon "correctness" eventually causes these restrictive congregations to implode upon themselves as they do not attract new members, and even their children become disillusioned with the absence of Christ's Spirit. Therefore, many of these churches are populated by an ever-increasing tendency toward a graying membership.

In order to avoid extinction, the Churches of Christ need to enact several changes in philosophy and action. Some churches have made these changes already and are growing at impressive rates. Other Churches of Christ, however, refuse to change and have actually disfellowshipped the churches with an inclusive philosophy. This situation is ironic, since the more inclusive churches not only reflect the original restoration principles but also the Spirit of Christ.

The first change the restrictive Churches of Christ need to make is to eliminate their spirit of exclusivity. Maintaining this spirit results in nothing more than maintaining the Churches of Christ as a secular organization. Evidence of this secularization is obvious by the often-given reason for refusing to make needed changes by saying, "If we do that, we will be just like the denominations."

A second orientation that presents problems for the Churches of Christ is the elders for life tradition, which has led to virtual dictatorships in the leadership of churches. These elders have tended to be overseers rather than shepherds. Having been an elder myself, I have experienced this attitude first hand hearing on more than one occasion the statement, "This is not a democracy," being made to circumvent the wishes of the congregation. I have seen this type of eldership totally quench the Spirit of Christ and drive it away from the body. Usually, in the absence of spiritual directiveness, a works orientation is substituted in order to instill at least an impression of doing God's will. As servants of the congregation, elders should be subject and accountable to the congregation. As Paul told Timothy, *"The elders who direct the affairs of the church well are worthy of double honor, especially those whose work is preaching and teaching. Those who sin are to be rebuked publicly, so that the others may take warning"* (I Timothy 5: 17, 20). Thus, the idea of accountability to God and to the congregation is set forth in this passage. As an evangelist, Paul told Timothy that it was his responsibility to rebuke the leadership in a public manner when sin was present. Clearly, this is a precarious position for any paid preacher, but it is also a responsibility of the position. Many inclusively oriented Churches of Christ have begun to appoint elders for specified terms of service, with the elder's needing to be reaffirmed by the congregation when his term is over. This orientation is as scriptural as the "elder for-life" appointment and instills much needed accountability to the position.

A third area of needed change is the restrictive role forced upon women by these churches. Although women taught, prayed, prophesied, and served in the New Testament, today's exclusive churches have limited women's roles to teaching the children and general service. Where are the scriptural prohibitions to women reading the word in the assembly, making announcements, leading singing, passing communion, and even wording prayers?

A fourth needed change is an increased focus upon the Holy Spirit and an intimate relationship with Christ instead of relying upon "head knowledge" about God. This focus has led to a "doing" rather than a "being" orientation towards God. It has caused these churches to focus upon the specifics of rituals with an emphasis to make sure that it is done just right in a "decent and orderly manner." In this search for perfection of action, many have forgotten the "being" part of our Christianity. Thus, God says, *"Be holy as I am holy"* (Leviticus 11: 44). However, it does not seem that God believes that we can achieve holiness by "doing" because he also says through Isaiah, *"All our righteous acts are like filthy rags"* (64: 6). Therefore, this holiness demanded by God can only be reached through life in Jesus and being Christlike. Unfortunately, both the Pharisee restorers and the modern exclusive Churches of Christ sought this perfection through doing exactly what they thought God demanded. It's sad that the only righteousness produced by this orientation toward God was, and still is, self-righteousness. This self-righteousness always causes increased distance between man and God and will never result in God's followers being transformed into the image of his son.

*–**Bill Chance** was born in Louisville, Kentucky, in 1946, and raised in southern Indiana. He grew up in the Church of Christ, and as an adult has served as deacon and elder in various congregations. Professionally, Bill is an Associate Professor of Surgery at the University of Cincinnati Medical Center. He holds M.A. and Ph.D. degrees in experimental psychology and has worked in research for the past 25 years. He recently returned to graduate school, earning a M.A. in community counseling. Bill is licensed as a Professional Counselor in Ohio and practices pastoral and parenting counseling part-time. His greatest desire is for the church that bears Jesus' name to also possess His Spirit and emulate His personality.*

Chapter 2
Beyond Tradition and Contemporary Worship

Then some of the Pharisees and teachers of the law came to Jesus from Jerusalem and asked, "Why do your disciples break the traditions of the elders? They don't wash their hands before they eat!"
Jesus replied, "And why do you break the command of God for the sake of your traditions? For God said, "Honor your father and mother and anyone who curses his father or mother must be put to death. But you say that if a man says to his father or mother, 'whatever help you might otherwise have received from me is a gift devoted to God, he is not to honor his father with it.' Thus you nullify the word of God for the sake of your tradition. You hypocrites! Isaiah was right when he prophesied about you:
These people honor me with their lips, but their hearts are far from me. They worship me in vain; their teachings are but rules taught by men"
(Matthew 15:1-9 NIV).

It wasn't a pair of dirty hands that troubled the Pharisees. Their fundamental concern was the failure of Jesus' disciples to observe the traditions of the elders who had legislated ceremonial hand washing as a mandatory religious requirement.[ix] Pharisaical leadership always reduces worship to a series of little rituals and ceremonies. Jesus and his disciples had ignored their legalist hand-washing requirement. With the unflappable ability to employ a question to offset the grace-stifling demands of legalism, Jesus asks, *"And why do you break the commands of God, for the sake of your traditions?"*

In case these Pharisees misunderstand, Jesus offers a concrete example of how scribal tradition becomes a higher authority than God when one violates the command to honor his father and mother. These separatists were without excuse because rabbinic tradition had recognized for centuries that honoring father and mother meant supporting them in old age, both physically and financially. But the priests had developed a well thought-out scam that not only violated the spirit of the fifth commandment but also contravened the letter of the written law. Their ploy aided the legalist by allowing him to make a vow to give to the temple and at the same time exempt him from honoring his parents with financial support. Once this 'corban' vow had been made, personal resources became temple assets.[x] It's at this point that Jesus quotes Isaiah's prophecy: *"They worship me in vain"* (Matthew 15:9).

Hand-Washing Rituals of the Twenty-First Century

Worship should always be contemporary in the sense that it is always being incarnated into the current cultural situation, yet reminiscent of two thousand years ago, traditions continue to threaten the progress of the body of Christ. It is unfortunate that a Christian community once known as a "people of the book" now finds it difficult to discern scripture from tradition.

I'm thinking of the life-long church member whose life's passion is policing the preacher's wardrobe every Sunday morning. I'm thinking of the mass exodus that is likely to occur the Sunday morning that leadership decides to replace the traditional twenty-minute sermon with a contemporary drama communicating the same saving message of Jesus.

My theory about these well-meaning pharisaical Christians is that the failure to develop, nurture, and grow a deep personal relationship with the living God has led to a "spiritual-intimacy void" that has forced them to channel all their energies in the direction of a "doing religion." It's a Christianity that is built on knowledge and rightness. When one exchanges the internal relational nature of the Christian life for an external religion (a doing religion), one soon elevates doctrine to the same status as the Gospel. Patternism soon follows and close behind is the tattered trail of censorious condemnation. Traditional Church of Christ hermeneutics and the "five acts of worship" become more important than the men and women Jesus died for two thousand years ago. If you doubt my analysis, let someone tamper with the status quo, and you have just touched the closest thing they know about God.

Songbooks or transparencies, drama or rational-centered preaching, hand clapping or no clapping is not the issue. These are simply the externals of a culture on a continuum of time expressing worship to a God who transcends the culture of our times.

Forward Looking

The demand for depth and substance reminds us of the need to find those biblical and transcultural principles of worship that have endured a two-thousand year history, then to incarnate these deep principles into a new style appropriate for the cultural patterns of a postmodern world. If we achieve this and remain unified, then the new generation will have taken us beyond the contemporary worship of yesterday into the contemporary worship of tomorrow.

Chapter 3
Diversity Is Biblical

The genius of the restoration plea is in its call for Christians to unite despite their many differences. Our movement's history, as well as the early church's history, is replete with examples of unity in diversity. The secret is simple. Rally around Jesus; agree on the essentials; allow for differences in non-essentials.

First-Century Diversity
In Romans 14, Paul addressed the diversity of the early church. Some would only eat vegetables; some wouldn't drink wine; others observed certain holy days. How did Paul handle the problem? Did he set them all straight with a rigid orthodox interpretation that demanded uniformity? No. He allowed each one the liberty to exercise his personal spiritual practice as long as these preferences weren't bound on others.

The New Testament emphasizes diversity. It is not wrong to remain single, but it is wrong to prohibit marriage (1 Timothy 4:3). It is not wrong to abstain, but it is wrong to forbid wine (Romans 14:21). John the Baptist was an abstemious loner who preferred the desert to parties and luxuries. His sermons emphasized doom and judgment. Jesus was the opposite. His sermons emphasized grace and mercy (Matthew 11:18-19). He was a party-goer, a gregarious friend of sinners. Yet both Jesus and John pleased God.

Early Restoration Diversity
J. W. McGarvey was opposed to instrumental music (although he opposed the instrument in the public assembly, he didn't oppose its use in Sunday school) and the missionary society.

Tolbert Fanning, the founder of the *Gospel Advocate*, supported the missionary society.

Moses Lard opposed instrumental music and the missionary society but believed in the premillennial reign of Christ. He was also a pacifist who fled to Canada to avoid the Civil War.

Barton Stone emphasized experience; Campbell emphasized rationality. Because Stone was unsure of the relationship within the Godhead and questioned the Trinity, he was accused of Arianism.[xi] Campbell believed the millennium was dawning and named his paper "The Millennial Harbinger."

T.B. Larimore preached anywhere, even for the instrumentalist churches. His reasoning was "the gospel is more important than the organ."

Present Restoration Diversity

Pass out three hundred questionnaires in your congregation next Sunday, and it will dispel any ideas you had on uniformity in the Churches of Christ. We have different views on deaconesses, marriage and divorce, hand clapping in the assembly, moderate use of alcohol, participation in community ministerial alliances, praise-teams, and women passing communion. Is it necessary that we all agree on the above issues before we worship and work together? If Christians with different understandings on these matters moved to the same city, they could form a congregation and work together in spite of their differences.

When Is Disfellowship Biblical?

In the New Testament, the following cases are the only ones that require a severing of fellowship:

- A denial of the incarnation of Jesus Christ (1 John 4:1-6).
- Rejecting biblical grace by relying upon human works as meritorious or supplemental to the sacrifice of Christ (Galatians 1:8-9).
- An immoral unrepentant lifestyle that openly flaunts God's will (1 Corinthians 5).
- A refusal to bear responsibility in practical matters (working for a living), which places a burden on the church (2 Thessalonians 3:6).
- An argumentative spirit which fractionalizes and destroys peace and harmony in the body of Christ (Titus 3:10).

Whenever believers embrace religion, they bury themselves in their compulsive doctrines. They become so entangled in the world of church dogma that they fail to retreat to the loving arms of God.

Jesus didn't come to bring religion, but life. Christ isn't a new Moses; Golgotha isn't a new Sinai; and the gospel isn't a new law with hundreds of codified "thou shalls" and "thou shall nots" (2 Corinthians 3:7-18). Religion murdered Christ, but He came to bring you life and relationship, despite individual diversities.

Chapter 4
History Primer 101

Pre-Modern Era: Superstition
Mythology. Pre-modern is generally before the eighteenth century and is also called pre-critical, since the prevailing mythological and superstitious attitudes went virtually unchallenged.

Modern Era: Reason
Demythologizing. The eighteenth century Enlightenment gave birth to a modern worldview based on scientific method. Modernity did away with superstition and myth and built Western civilization on the blueprint of fact and reason.

Postmodern Era: Intuition
Re-mythologizing. Post-modernity is a reaction to the exalted position modernity has given to reason and science. In a postmodern world, reason and intuition are equally valid in determining truths. In the mind of a postmodern person, there is no such thing as absolute truth. For Christian leaders grappling in a postmodern world, the assuredness of Christian hegemony is fractured by openness to all world religions.

The emerging Churches of Christ must seek to communicate Jesus Christ as The Way, The Truth, and The Life amid the challenges of this postmodern world.

Chapter 5
Star Trek Primer 101

Stanley Grenz, in the first chapter of *A Primer on Postmodernism*, illustrates the difference between modernism and postmodernism by comparing and contrasting the two series *Star Trek* and *Star Trek: the Next Generation*. In the first series, the crew of Starship Enterprise, from different human backgrounds, all worked together for the good of humanity. One of the heroes was Spock (half-human, half-Vulcan), who illustrated the perfect ideal of the modern man: he solved all problems by rational thought and was not swayed by emotions or any sense of the transcendent or mystical. The second series, *Star Trek: The Next Generation*, had a crew from much more diverse backgrounds, including non-humans. The rational input is from an android machine, *Data*, which longs to be human with human emotions. There is much emphasis on the transcendent, and more attention is given to emotions and feelings. Rationality alone is no longer enough to solve problems. *Counsellor Troi* is a woman who has the gift of knowing peoples' emotions and is an important member of the crew. The presence of other life forms means that humans are no longer the center of the universe, only a minor part.

Identifying more with *Data*, young people today feel more like machines who don't know how to have relationships but desperately long for them and for a sense of community which most of their families don't provide.

Modernism is like Captain Kirk's going out to conquer and subdue the "final frontier, where no man has gone before." Postmodernism is like Captain Picard guiding his politically-correct crew through space with the goal of reconciling and making the galaxy a safe place to live (unlike Captain Kirk's space quest of conquer and triumph). Most postmodern people are like Captain Picard. They go to all extremes to avoid any potentially painful conflict because it's a reminder of the conflict they experienced in the emotionally scarred homes they grew up in. Reconciling is more important than conquering.

To characterize postmodernism would be to label it as a different (from modernism) and subjective experiential way of looking at the world. Unfortunately, it has left this novel culture with a deep skepticism for all moral, absolute, and universal truths.

No longer can the truths of Christianity be tied to the traditional approaches (Captain Kirk generation) of another era. We must move forward. If we don't move forward, this untraditional generation (Data generation) will walk in another direction.

The Original *Star Trek* and The *Next Generation* Appeal to Different Audiences

A healthy church that reaches out to its generation (Captain Kirk generation) will attract Treckies of like kind. But there is a large generation of young people who find the values and ambitions of Captain Kirk and the mission of the original Enterprise irrelevant. That's why *Star Trek: The Next Generation* was created. *Star Trek* re-runs were not attracting the younger audience. Likewise, the boomer-oriented churches, that operate more on the values of modern thinking, aren't attracting the postmodern culture. That doesn't mean there is anything wrong with modernist baby-boomer focused churches; it just means that they aren't attracting young people whose world view and values are radically different than the predominant ones of the generation which preceded them.

Here are a few reasons why:

- **Most postmodern seekers, particularly young people, believe in an impersonal God and human superficiality.** With the exception of atheists and deists, many modernist thinkers don't follow a personal God but would tell you that they still believe in a deity. Alcoholics Anonymous capitalized on this years ago in naming Him a "higher power." This is less exclusive than "God," but in its own way just as personal. Postmodern people tend to believe more in the Eastern concept of God as an impersonal life force in all people and things. Part of the reason for the resurgence of *Star Wars: The Next Generation* was due to a generation of young people who easily accepted and longed to experience the Eastern concept of *The Force* in these movies. This impersonal God concept has also lead many postmoderns to give up the modern thinking of people evolving to a better or higher state. The cynicism of postmodernism has led many to believe that humans are actually no more inherently valuable than, say, animals or trees. Perhaps you can see already the immense challenge for the church here...and why quoting Bible verses as authoritative proof to a postmodern young person means nothing and that modern, deductive, or logical arguments against things like abortion or mercy-killing fall on deaf ears.

- **Most postmodern seekers are much more community minded.** Modern thinkers are individualists. The Marlboro Man is the modern prototype. His rugged individualism is the personification of the modernist's belief in self. Interestingly, the postmodern person is not attractive to this modern individualism portrayed by the Marlboro Man. In contrast, the appeal is to the group of friends who do life together on *Seinfeld* or *Friends* or *E.R.* where community looks like the family they wish they had experienced in real life. Because many young people today believe that you cannot define your own identity apart from some sense of community, they consider all truth and identity as socially constructed, not individually created. When a church recognizes this and builds with that in mind, it can become a tool powerfully used by God to bring a biblical sense of community to a generation longing for it but not knowing where to experience it. It's important that emerging churches begin building a church community where this generation of seekers can know one another and be known by others, where they can love and be loved, encourage and be encouraged, forgive and be forgiven, and bless and be blessed. This kind of community will be attractive to all people but essential in reaching and caring for postmodern seekers.

- **Most postmodern seekers are much more existentialist.** Modern thinkers believe that there are certain essential elements in human nature. For example, a modern secularist would argue that homosexuality was valid because some people are born that way, that it is their essential nature. However, most postmodernists don't care about such reasoning. They assert that any claims of essential nature are oppressive. They would argue that homosexuality is valid because there are no absolutes or essentials of identity and behavior anyway, that everyone is free to choose as he pleases... as long as his choice doesn't hurt someone else. The church cannot address these kinds of moral issues today the way it has in the past and expect to be heard or even understood. We can't make assumptions about what people know about God, the Bible, or about the church, for that matter. We must find common ground and begin working relationally with people to help them grow in their understanding of God's ways.

- **Most postmodern seekers are mystical.** Whereas modernists eliminated any credibility given to mystical experiences that could not be empirically established, most postmodern young people in particular are very open to the supernatural world, changes in consciousness, and mystical experiences. They are open to multiple ways of knowing. In some cases, rationalism is seen as an inferior way of knowing. Therefore, a church which continues to produce only rational defenses for the veracity of the Bible, the deity of Christ or His bodily resurrection, will find itself speaking only to the already convinced but never reaching the younger generations of people and seekers who don't care about these things, even if they are true, because they don't readily see what difference they make to their lives. We are a generation of pragmatists. We care more about if something works than if it is true. Postmodern young people process truth or information relationally rather than propositionally. They don't respond well to intellectual apologetics as a starter. Deductive and logical truth is important but not nearly as important as relationship and real-life evidence in the form of experience. A young person will say, "Let me see this in your life before you try to tell it to me with your words." Not too bad, considering the apostle Paul said, "Follow me as I follow Christ." In other words, follow my example. Live as I live. Paul invited people to look at his life to see if he was practicing what he preached. We should be prepared to do likewise.

Postmodernism is the single most powerful force in shaping the mindset, attitudes, and values of this new era. If the church is going to understand and minister to this generation, postmodernity must be its starting point. How this generation and following generations analyze and process truth will change the way we communicate and reason with people. The old modern, rational, Captain-Kirk style of preaching and teaching must be modified and replaced with new approaches of telling the "old, old story."

Chapter 6
Forty-four Reasons Churches of Christ Don't Change

1. We've never done it before.
2. Nobody else has ever done it.
3. It has never been tried before.
4. We tried it before.
5. Another congregation tried it before.
6. The denominations are doing it.
7. We've been doing it this way for 25 years.
8. It won't work in a small church.
9. It won't work in a large church.
10. It won't work at our congregation.
11. We're doing all right as it is.
12. The elders will never buy it.
13. It needs further investigation.
14. The other congregations are not doing it.
15. It's too much trouble to change.
16. Our church is different.
17. The minister says it can't be done.
18. The elders say it can't be done.
19. The members won't like it.
20. The deacons say it can't be done.
21. The worship leader says it can't be done.
21. It can't be done.
22. We don't have the money.
23. We don't have brotherhood support.
24. We'll be marked.
25. It's too visionary.
26. You can't teach an old dog new tricks.
27. It's too radical a change.
28. We don't have the time.
29. Membership won't buy it.
30. It's contrary to Scripture
31. It's contrary to the way the Church of Christ does things.

32. It will cost too much.
33. It's not our problem.
34. I don't like it.
35. You're right, but ....
36. We're not ready for it.
37. It needs more thought.
38. We can't take the chance.
39. Let's form a committee.
40. It needs committee study.
41. The Church of Christ across town won't like it.
42. It needs sleeping on.
43. It won't work in this church.
44. It's impossible.

Chapter 7
Change-Agent Development

Ask a leader involved in any area of life and he will undoubtedly agree that the implementation of change almost always is accompanied by strain, pressure, and moments of anxiety. There's something innate within the human condition that rebels against the disruption of what is safe and familiar. We laud the great restoration pioneers of the past for their ability to envision beyond what anyone at that specific time could fathom. We forget that visionaries often pay a tremendous price. Change rarely comes without exacting cost.

Christopher Columbus ignited a firestorm of controversy when he asked government officials to help him sail around the world. Certain that the earth was flat, the power brokers were in no mood for anything earthshaking. In Spain, he found people who risked testing his "round-earth" theory by financing his trip and, in turn, reaped a tremendous financial windfall. More importantly, because of Columbus' willingness to forge ahead amid the protests, our world was changed forever. The lesson: change can be both rewarding and risky.

It's not much different within the church. Every church leader would like to bring about successful change without generating too much controversy. It's no surprise, then, that change must be approached in a responsible manner.

Successfully implementing change within a congregation will always be demanding. This is understood, but it's possible to make changes with only minor resistance if leaders understand the critical skills necessary to move a congregation forward.

Legitimate Fear

Fear is a critical component in changing an individual's behavior. On the other hand, too much fear can paralyze individuals and churches. Balancing the mix of fear on an on-going basis becomes the critical skill of a change agent. A fear that is certainly legitimate, and one that should be expressed, is that churches who refuse to speak the "heart language" of their culture face the real possibility of becoming antiquated.

Often times the success of a change agent is based on how he delivers his message as much as the message he delivers. In a changing environment, the opportunity for misunderstanding is widespread. Clarity and consistency are key skills of change agents.

Resistance to the Movement

When church leaders talk about "dealing with resistance to change," their words sometimes conjure up the image of Christians being herded like cattle toward a destination they don't understand. We've implied that those who show signs of "resistance" are like stragglers who need to be brought back into line with a shout or a whack.

This type of thinking is wrong. People don't robotically resist innovative progress—but they do react to change that is imposed upon them arbitrarily and without consultation. Rather than "herding" people, a much more effective approach is for the leaders to build a clear vision of where the church needs to go in order to survive and be successful, then they need to responsibly share the vision and explain why the church's survival depends upon moving in a forward direction.

Rather than becoming preoccupied with stragglers, church leaders should focus on providing support and encouragement for the enthusiasts. These people will lead the way, act as role models, and mark a path for others to follow. Supportive approach is the first step in making people part of the solution rather than part of the problem.

Reachable Objectives

When churches don't believe they can meet an objective, the membership becomes disenchanted, but if vision casting has been articulated and framed with reachable goals, churches will feel challenged to turn their vision into reality. Often the same set of circumstances communicated in a different way will determine whether the outcome is success or failure.

The day-to-day implementers need to have special skills to listen, negotiate, and persuade the membership to make the key changes for success. It is essential that a network of change agents subsist with the common goal of reaching an ever-changing culture for Christ.

Chapter 8
Nine Tips for Change Agents

Everyone who understands the necessity of upgrading ministry to stay abreast of the changing times would do well to carry a business card that reads, "I am a learner." Not only would the phrase keep us humble, but it would also remind us that we are disciples of the greatest change agent the world has ever seen, Jesus Christ.

The word *disciple* has a non-hierarchical "ring," yet there are some important reminders for the disciple to remember when initiating change within a congregation. Here are nine lessons for would-be change agents:

- **Be open to change at the start.** Even if you think you know what you're doing, chances are you don't know what you could be doing. Open up your mind to as much new thinking as you can absorb. You may find different and better ideas than the ones your congregation has settled into.
- **Network like crazy.** There is a network of church leaders across America who, like you, have either been thinking change or have already made changes. I've found you can get in touch with them easily. At times someone says, "I can't believe you talked with so-and-so! How'd you do it?" The answer I give them is, "I called him."
- **Freethinking and brainstorming.** Create a matrix of ideas from the freethinking leaders in your congregation. Then document two categories of thinking – the elements of a growing and changing church and the pitfalls to avoid.
- **Take leadership along.** Visit congregations that have taken innovative approaches to church growth. In the beginning some will be skeptical. Take them on

benchmarking trips to show them other churches are actually making some of the same changes.
- **No fear!** You've got to be fearless and not worry about the churches that have made the decision that change is unbiblical and that stagnation is scriptural.
- **Be a learning person yourself.** Change agents have to be in love with learning and changing, but just as important is the communication that must take place between the change agent and the body of Christ. Cast your vision before the people in nearly every message, but be able to demonstrate that the vision comes directly off the pages of Scripture. If you're doing an expository study, seek to find pieces of the vision in every scripture. Don't hesitate to point them out!
- **Laugh when it hurts.** Helping a church "to transition" can be demanding and sometimes discouraging work. Keep a good sense of humor. It also helps if you've got another leader that can pray with you when things aren't going well.
- **Know the make-up of the church before you try to change anything.** It's impossible to do the work of a change agent if you're just a theorist. It's essential that you know the people you worship with as well as their talents and potentials; otherwise, you'll not be successful in creating a change strategy. Understand the people!
- **Finish what you start.** Starting without finishing is the "black hole" of change and progress. You must determine early on that you are not going to be part of a second-rate operation.
- **Expect God to come through.** Remember the time Paul was shipwrecked on Malta and bitten by a snake? God came through! Remember the time Moses faced an ocean in front of him and an army behind him? God came through! Remember the time Daniel was on the lion's menu? God came through! Remember Abraham, Joseph, Gideon, Elijah, and all the others in the ranks of faith? God came through!

Chapter 9
Implementing Change

The grace-oriented churches of Christ are mystified by the strange, out-of-date traditions that the mainline congregations continue to elevate to the level of scripture: "hundreds-of-years-old" music, strange seats, rational-centered preaching, and a religious language that confuses the populace, yet many within cry, "No change!" None of these vestiges speak to the "heart language" of today's contemporary culture. At its worst, it bores and alienates the unchurched, yet the church refuses to change! Culture rolls forward, but the church's anthem is the same, "As it was in the beginning, it is now, and it shall forever be."

Unfortunately, there are some churches that have gone beyond the liberties of scripture by changing the foundational doctrines of the Bible. But even then, they often continue to refuse change in structural and cultural areas. This is the worst-case scenario—changing the things we should never change but holding fast to the things we should be willing to change.

Biblical Example

The book of Acts documents the struggle between the Holy Spirit and the frail humans who tried to lead God's people in the first century. Over and over again, God tried to move out through the church to reach the masses outside the enclaves of the saved, but he was met by hyper-conservative, foot-dragging Christian believers who were not willing to change. Acts 10 and 11 are some of the clearest passages on this unfortunate tendency. Luke goes to great lengths to demonstrate that God practically had to thrash Peter into preaching to Cornelius and his household in Acts 10. Three times Peter answered God's command with the odd and self-contradictory formula, "No, never Lord." What provoked such a spirit of resistance in Peter? God was calling him to change.

Once Peter finally obeyed, his charming greeting to his eager audience was, "You know it is not lawful for a Jew to enter a gentile's house." Notice Peter, like most traditionalists, had lost track of what was biblically "lawful" through the blindness of his out-dated, selfish tradition. The Old Testament never said Jews couldn't enter a gentile's home, and countless gentiles may have been deprived of biblical witness because of this preposterous, hyper-protective tradition.

Nevertheless, Peter carried out his mission and the entire household was converted. Afterward, the brothers in Jerusalem called him on the carpet, accusing him of sin for visiting a gentile. A long, seven point defense follows in Chapter 11 of Acts, including a complete repetition of the vision already described in Chapter 10, and citations of scripture, as well as the words of Christ. Luke is again at pains to indicate how difficult this transition was.

Finally, even these stubborn ones were convinced, admitting, *"God has granted even the gentiles repentance leading to life"* (Acts 11:18). But it's impossible to mistake the next comment juxtaposed to their admission. Verse 19 declares that *"those who had been scattered. . . traveled as far as Phoenicia, Cypress, and Antioch, telling the message only to Jews."* What a shocking statement! Is it possible that even after such a convincing episode, they still had not changed? Yes, only a few radicals were nutty enough to preach even to gentiles, and they wound up in the city of Antioch (verse 20).

Eventually, the center of God's activity shifted from Jerusalem (which was still mired in the old skins according to Acts 21) to Antioch because they were more willing to change.

Jesus warned that old wineskins become rigid and brittle. They will not flex enough to contain his new wine. He also added the comment, "No one, after drinking the old wine wants the new," for he says, "the old is better."

Application to Today

God has a terrible time convincing his followers that change is an essential and never-ending need in the church. What is wrong with leaders who call for change all the time? Nothing at all! There will never be a time when substantial, sweeping changes will not be necessary. When we feel dismayed by leaders perennially calling for change, we are subconsciously thinking, "If we made the right decisions in the first place, we wouldn't have to change." But this simply isn't true. No decision is so correct that it removes the need for subsequent change. With culture and the church's membership constantly changing, that which was culturally right one decade will likely be culturally wrong the next decade.

A church that will not change has erected an idol that offends the character of God. Jesus said, *"You have a fine way of setting aside the commands of God in order to observe your own traditions!"* (Mark 7:9). In our fleshly efforts to control our environment, to derive a false sense of security from the "sameness" of our surroundings, we have put our personal comfort ahead of the needs of lost people outside the church. God is not pleased, and he will move on to find another group that is willing to change to do his bidding.

Difficulties Caused by Change

How can we justify a leadership who has called for changes that have led to problems? To this I answer that change will lead to problems from time to time. The severity of the problems have to be weighed over time, evaluating the wisdom of given leaders. However, anyone who wants an error-proof system is also insisting on a change-proof system. As soon as we refuse to take chances, we're at the same time refusing to follow God.

Christian leaders can unwillfully lead people in the wrong direction, simply by overlooking attendant problems. The realization that real people sometimes get hurt because someone made a bad decision is part of the sometimes sickening burden of leadership. However, this doesn't negate the fact that leadership should continue moving forward by implementing responsible change. The menace of not changing, even in the face of ineffectiveness, is worse than anything we will face as the result of carefully considered change.

Chapter 10
Baby Dedications

Last week a church and a local elementary school said goodbye to a principal and a Christian. When the news of Jim's death reached his friends and family, it became very personal to each hearer. That's the way it happens. Death requires the funeral of a love one to bring us to a point where we realize the stark finality of our loss.

Jim was a special brother and friend to many. He was a courageous man, dedicated to both his family and the children he loved.

I will miss Jim, but before he left this world, he taught me a lot about how to enter the "passageway" that all must enter at the close of life. What did I learn? First, I learned how to die courageously. Jim never gave up, and he never complained or expressed a doubt. Secondly, and maybe more importantly, he left this world *dedicated* to his family and to the children he taught and loved. The interim principal expressed this when she said, "The kids flocked around Jim on the playground. Jim was a *dedicated* professional who cared about the children."

Being dedicated to the people we love requires two things:

- That we love the people to whom we are dedicating ourselves and that we believe in the pledge of our commitment.
- That we persevere and practice consistency.

Maybe if we were as serious in dedicating our children to the Lord as Jim was to the children at his elementary school, the front door of the church wouldn't be the exit door for so many of our kids.

Our children are a gift from God, and there's no greater human experience and responsibility a husband and wife can enter into than raising a child in the Lord.

The joy of it all, however, must be encased in the responsibility and knowledge that the child has indeed come from God and that the Lord has given specific instructions to parents on how to raise their children. In Deuteronomy 6:6-7 the Lord says, *"These commandments that I give you today are to be upon your hearts. Impress them on your children. Talk about them when you sit at home and when you walk along the road, when you lie down and when you get up"* (NIV). Ephesians 6:4 also says, *"Do not exasperate your children; instead, bring them up in the training and instruction of the Lord"* (NIV).

All Christian parents, through prayer and commitment, should dedicate themselves to successfully raising their children to know Jesus. But let's take it a step further with the challenge of making the commitment a public one. Why? Because it's a well-known truth that when one goes public with a promise, he is much more likely to stay with his vow. Dedicating a child to the Lord is not baptismal sacrament or a salvation ceremony. It's simply a public acknowledgement and pledge that parents will:

- Bring their child up in the nurture and admonition of the Lord.
- Teach them scripture that will lead them to know Jesus as Lord.
- Recognize and encourage their talents and uniqueness.
- Love them as Jesus loves us.

The purpose of baby dedication is instituted in the intention of the parent or parents. When parents publicly dedicate their baby, they're acknowledging their willingness to stay with the commitment. So the ceremony is more a time of dedication for the parents than it is for the baby. One day that child will be called upon to make his/her own decision for the Lord; this act by the parents in no way negates or makes unnecessary that later act when the child reaches the age when he/she decides for or against the Lord.

Public Vows

We make public vows when we marry by calling our friends, relatives, and loved ones to witness our vows. Why not do the same when we bring a precious soul into the world? Instead of publicly vowing to "love, honor and obey," we vow, as a couple, to give ourselves to the godly rearing of our child, while simultaneously calling upon our loved ones not only to witness our pledge but to aid us in carrying it through.

Is this a biblical idea? You bet it is! We have the precedent for baby dedication established through the presentation of Samuel by Hannah (1 Samuel 1:28) and of Jesus by Joseph and Mary (Luke 2:22).

Baby dedications also afford the opportunity to invite unsaved friends and family to the church. They may never have accepted your invitation to an assembly of Christians in the past, but the odds increase when their grandchild makes a public appearance at church. As a result, you'll not only be promising to raise your child in a Christian home, but you'll also be planting the Gospel seed in the hearts of those visiting.

I know some of you are wondering if there is authority for a baby dedication ceremony in a worship service. Since the term "worship service" and assembly rules are conspicuously absent in the New Testament, Christians are free to do anything that is "decent and in order" and that edifies the assembled group.

Chapter 11
Prohibition Theology

A few years ago, I attended a wedding at a Greek Orthodox Church. My Palm Pilot told me that I shouldn't stay for the reception, but the wedding was so unusual I decided to stay for a look. Uncertain as to what I might find in the basement of this ornate edifice, I descended the stairs anticipating a dozen different possibilities. Mystery was about to unfold as I moved closer to the fellowship hall. Slowly, I made my way through the line until I came to the entrance door where the officiating priest greeted me with a left-handed handshake. An eight-ounce Little King beer occupied his right hand. Gaily he welcomed me to the reception and then pointed me to a crowd of people in a corner who had surrounded what seemed to be the reception's hub. I walked over to an ice chest where the preponderance of guests had congregated. I watched as they engaged in the mastery of brewage.

Today, a decade later, this event still takes the award as the "all-time winner of the most unusual wedding reception." I've thought about this group of believers who not only drank alcohol but also served it to the public. Needless to say, they've challenged my "prohibition" theology, which necessitated that I take a closer look at scripture and the cultural influences that have molded my beliefs.

More recently, I've become familiar with a group of believers (a community church) who not only believe in drinking in moderation, but also purchase alcohol for their small group fellowships. (It's amazing how many outsiders come to their meetings.)

I don't think I would stir controversy by saying that wine was given to us by a beneficent God who knew from time to time that we would need it. The Bible has a lot to say about wine. In fact, the grapevine and its primary product, wine, are mentioned more than any other plant.

Wine's Abbreviated History

After the Great Flood, Noah, a man of the soil, starts over by planting a vineyard and making wine. He is credited as being the first to plant a vineyard. Lamech, Noah's father, said that Noah would "bring us relief and comfort from our work and the toil of our hands."[xii]

With the first wine came the first occasion of drunkenness. The Bible warns of the dangers of too much wine. It declares wine is a mocker and whoever is led astray by it, is not wise. On the other side of the same coin, it reminds us God made the wine that gladdens the heart of man. Clearly, moderation is called for here.

The Bible doesn't say a great deal about the use of wine in ordinary life. It was customary to present wine to travelers. Paul recommended wine to Timothy as a digestive aid. It was used at feasts and marriages. In times of scarcity it was mixed with water and sometimes even with milk. Its importance is evident in the fact that God, as a punishment, deprived Israel of it.

Of the above-mentioned Bible stories, the most controversial, if not the most interesting is the story that came out of Cana.

Three days later there was a wedding in the village of Cana in Galilee. Jesus' mother was there. Jesus and his disciples were guests also. When they started running low on wine at the wedding banquet, Jesus' mother told him, "They're just about out of wine."

Jesus said, "Is that any of our business, Mother—yours or mine? This isn't my time. Don't push me."

She went ahead anyway, telling the servants, "Whatever he tells you, do it."

Six stoneware water pots were there, used by the Jews for ritual washings. Each had twenty to thirty gallons. Jesus ordered the servants, "Fill the pots with water." And they filled them to the brim.

"Now fill your pitchers and take them to the host," Jesus said, and they did.

When the host tasted the water that had become wine (he didn't know what had just happened but the servants, of course, knew), he called out to the bridegroom, "Everybody I know begins with their finest wines and after the guest have had their fill brings in the cheap stuff. But you've saved the best till now!"

The act in Cana of Galilee was the first sign Jesus gave, the first glimpse of his glory. And his disciples believed in him.

After this he went down to Capernaum along with his mother, brothers, and disciples, and stayed several days. [xiii]

The party has been drinking wine to the point that the host has completely run out and is on the verge of being embarrassed. From a comment made later in the account (verse 10), we know that the guests have not restricted themselves to a few discreet sips in a toast to the bride. It is clear that they have been doing some serious celebration because they have reached the point where they'll not recognize the difference between a good wine and a mediocre wine. It's under these conditions that Mary asks Jesus to do something about the problem.

Before we examine Jesus' response, consider for a moment the response of a prohibitionist in this dilemma. First, it is doubtful that he would be at a wedding reception where wine was flowing freely. Second, it is doubtful that he would stay if the drinking were as concerted as is indicated in the story, but if he did, what would be his probable response when asked to provide more wine for already tipsy guests? It is unlikely that he would agree to replenish the supply, by means natural or supernatural.

Jesus, however, not only replenished the supply, he made an additional 120 to 180 gallons.[xiv] Not only does this behavior contradict everything we have ever heard from prohibitionists, it causes us to re-evaluate the conventional understanding of the proper limit of drinking.

I certainly know the dangers of drinking, both privately and publicly, and this may be reason enough to discount my thoughts on the wedding Jesus attended almost two thousand years ago in Cana, but I can't help but wonder if we've denied Christians the scriptural freedom to drink within moderation?

Chapter 12
Worship and Emotions

Late one night, my wife was awakened by a phone call. A hospital emergency room nurse told her that our daughter had been injured in an automobile accident. She said that we should come to the hospital at once. I have to admit that I was scared. My frustration continued to build during the frenzied drive to the hospital. As we waited to consult with the emergency room doctor about the extent of the injuries, I began to notice emotions that I had never felt in the past. Eventually, the doctor came and told us that our daughter had broken three dorsal vertebrae in her spine.

Waves of emotional reactions were interspersed with periods of numbness. I felt out of control, yet I maintained my composure by taking care of the immediate needs I recognized. I talked with the radiologist and I called relatives.

From early childhood, males are taught that men should protect their families. Fathers are responsible for fulfilling their wife's and children's physical, financial, and emotional needs. They are to be in control, to be strong (never scared), and capable of fixing all things. By adulthood, males are catapulted into stereotypical roles. Often they feel torn while trying to fulfill the roles expected of them. Showing emotions is labeled as weak or pitiful. They are expected to be strong under adverse circumstances, even when there's an automobile accident involving a daughter they love.

It's easy to ignore and eventually deny your feelings with the consuming responsibilities and demands of a busy life. But being the analytical type that I am (is this a male thing?), I've often wondered if this is the reason I am hesitant to show and express my feelings.

Feelings and Worship

If worship is a response of the whole person to God, then we cannot ignore emotions. When we worship we think about Christ and contemplate His character. We're invited to express our brokenness, gratitude, awe, fear, joy, and humility before God. Worship calls forth a language of the heart. It's communion with God, and our response should produce an outflow of feelings.

These feelings can be expressed in various ways. Some Christians clap their hands in rhythm to the music; although, those of us who are rhythmically challenged would rather sit on them. Some raise their hands when they pray or worship. These are but two of the ways we express our feelings toward God.

The raising of hands is certainly one of the biblically sanctioned postures of prayer, but not the only one. There are numerous positions that the Bible acknowledges as appropriate for prayer and worship. One can sit, kneel, stand, lie prostrate, or raise hands receptively toward God while realizing that none of these postures makes one more spiritual or his worship more acceptable. These are simply human ways of inclining ourselves to the living God, a way of bringing our physical posture in line with our spiritual desire. Such actions can be helpful for us in our prayer lives and worship experiences.

Recently, I had a conversation with a worship leader from a congregation in Ohio. He provided me with a good set of connections between the physical posture in raising hands during worship and the mental/spiritual processes that might well accompany them.

Think about what position your arms would be in if you were standing and offering a bulky, but not necessarily heavy, gift to someone. Your arms would be outstretched shoulder width (or further apart), perhaps waist high, with your palms up. When you're worshipping/singing and "offering" yourself or your gifts to Christ, your hands and arms could be in this position.

Imagine that you see someone near and dear across the room that you haven't seen in a long while. When you invite them to embrace you, your outstretched arms will be raised probably almost to shoulder level, your hands open and palms up. Again, when you are worshipping/singing and wanting to "embrace" your Savior as friend and brother, your hands and arms could be in this position.

Now, think about what you would do with your hands if someone pointed a high-powered rifle at you, and you didn't want them to shoot you. Your arms would go up at least to shoulder height and your palms would be facing forward in the universal sign of surrender. In our worship, we can physically show our attitude of "surrender" to Jesus by raising our hands and declaring our vulnerability (We are weak, but He is strong).

Lifting the hands is just a way of reaching up to God to exalt Him or seek Him. It is perfectly appropriate. Some are concerned that this practice might be the early introduction of a charismatic theology for the Church of Christ. Raising hands in worship in no way embraces a charismatic theology any more than kneeling while praying embraces Catholic theology. The question shouldn't be is it "charismatic," but is it biblical?

The Use of Hands in Worship

The Bible not only permits the hand raising posture in prayer and worship but it also seems to encourage it (Psalm 28:2; 63:4; 134:2; 1Timothy 2:8). If you feel led to do this in your prayer life or in public worship, feel free to do so. But those who aren't moved to do the same are not required.

Clapping hands is a legitimate part of the worship experience (Psalm 47:1). It's a sign of enthusiasm and excitement, something we should have regarding the greatness of the living God. Sometimes our worship leaders will encourage clapping. This is fine. It's not something that has to be done all the time or by everyone, but it is certainly an appropriate aspect of responding to God. However, just as we sometimes clap and express enthusiasm, there will be times when we will be still and quiet expressing reverence.

Clapping or raising hands in worship shouldn't be a major worship issue. It is merely part of permitting a free and spontaneous response to the glory and greatness of God. One of the important things about life in the body of Christ is learning to discern between the mountains and the molehills or between the majors and the minors. This "hands" business is clearly one of the molehills.

In 1834, John Rogers wrote a letter to Alexander Campbell expressing his concern that the people of the restoration churches had become imbalanced. He wrote, "Many of us in running away from the extreme of enthusiasm, have on the other hand, passed the temperate zone and gone far into the frozen regions. There is, in too many churches, a cold-hearted, lifeless formality that freezes the energies." Even Campbell, who championed a rational approach to Christianity, raised similar concerns on several occasions. "Christianity certainly is an intellectual matter," he wrote in 1837, "but religion dwelling in the heart, rooted in the feelings and affections, is living, active, and a real existence....This is Christianity all the rest is machinery."

John Rogers' and Alexander Campbell's concern is as significant today as it was in the nineteenth century. Consequently, I've decided I'm going to oil my machinery before we assemble next Lord's Day and give my emotions the permission and freedom to emerge from the closet they've been closed up in.

Watch for me. I'll be the one with hands raised high, as I exalt the God of the universe. Will you join me?

Chapter 13
The World Waits

Shame is a normal human emotion that gives us the permission to be human. It defines our limits and keeps us within our human boundaries, reminding us that we can and will make mistakes. Healthy shame is the psychological foundation of humility, but healthy shame can be transformed into shame as a state of being. When this happens, shame takes over one's whole identity. To have shame as an identity is to believe that one's being is flawed, that one is defective as a human being. Once shame is transformed into an identity, it becomes toxic and dehumanizing.

There are many within the pages of the Bible who struggled with dysfunction: David, Absalom, Adam, Eve, and Solomon, just to name a few. But there is one woman in scripture whose story embodies them all, a story of abuse, failure, and shame. More importantly, it's a story of grace.

Shame Meets Grace In A Courtyard

They shove him out of the way and hiss, "Disappear!" Hurriedly, they grab her by the arm, push the door open and make their way down the alley toward the temple, disrupting the dawn. Weeping and shouting can be heard across the courtyard. They throw her into the middle of the crowd that has gathered to hear Jesus teach.

Confused and sweaty from the struggle, she sits in the sand bracing herself with arms behind her. She looks Jesus in the eyes. Her lips are pressed. The furrows on her forehead reveal her self-disgust.

The Pharisees are dressed in their smug self-righteousness. They're the "religious custodians of conduct," the self-appointed guardians of the faith.

"Adulteress!" they charged. "We caught her in the act!"

Strange circumstances. Jesus has been teaching and this woman has been cheating; these religious leaders are out to get them both.

"Teacher, this woman has been caught in the act." Their statement conjures up images of doors being kicked open and covers being jerked back. This woman had been removed from her private passion to be made a public spectacle. She has nowhere to hide. She's forced to face the shame of her illicit moment. From this day on she will be known as the neighborhood adulteress. Her sin will be on the lips of the market gossips.

Her act was both immoral and shameful, and now her remorse is unbearable. She has sinned against her husband and God. But the greater travesty in this moral mess almost goes unnoticed. The Pharisees have a despicable plan.

- The Law said that adultery was punishable by death. But only if two or more people witnessed the act. Question: What are the chances that two people accidentally stumbled upon a flurry of forbidden passion?
- Where was the second-half of this guilty party? It takes two to commitment adultery. Why wasn't the man marched out into the streets with this woman?

This was a first-century sting operation, and the woman was a dispensable part of the plan. She was the bait, a pawn in the Pharisee's hands. So with stones clenched tight they ask, "The Law of Moses commands us to stone such women. What do you say?"

The silence is deafening. The drama is intense.

The same finger that engraved the Ten Commandments on rock begins to write in the sand of a courtyard. What was He writing?[xv] I'm not sure, and neither are the scholars. Maybe He was writing the names of everyone who was holding a rock. Or maybe He was writing their sins in the dirt. Or perhaps He was writing just two words. NOT GULITY!

"Anyone here who has not sinned, you have the privilege of throwing the first stone...." At that moment the older men in the crowd looked to the younger. And the younger looked to the older, and then they looked at their lives. All that could be heard was the thud of twelve rocks and the shuffling of feet.

Jesus and the woman are left alone in this courtyard turned courtroom. The jury is gone. The woman looks in the face of Jesus expecting condemnation. Jesus continues writing, looks up and asks, "Where are your accusers? Is there anyone here that condemns you?"

"No Sir."

"Then neither do I condemn you, go now and sin no more" (John 8:11).

Throwing Stones

When George Barna, a Christian statistician, polled a sampling of non-Christians with the question, "What do you think about Christians?" He received the following top responses:

1. They go to church more than I do.
2. They are judgmental.

Sometimes we forget the truth about ourselves, and when we do, our righteousness becomes self-righteous, and our Christian witness is exchanged for the Pharisaical art of rock slinging. I have a Christian friend who has a rock mounted on a plaque with the inscription, *"First Stone"* (John 8:7). He keeps it on his desk as a reminder.

My sin is not the same as the woman who makes her living on the street. But I need the grace of God just as much as the woman "caught in the act." And so do you. Often Christians forget about the rock they crawled out from under on the day God looked them in the eye and said, "Neither do I condemn you, go now and sin no more."

> "When you get to Heaven you will likely view
> many folks whose presence there will be a shock to you.
> But do not be astonished, do not even stare,
> doubtless, there will be many folks surprised to
> see you there."

I don't know what happened to the woman in John 8. Maybe she went back to her husband. Maybe she became a disciple of Christ. Maybe she didn't. But what I do know is that Jesus loved her in the middle of her failure and shame. A Savior stood up for her when others wanted to stone her. He sent her on her way. "Neither do I condemn you, go now and sin no more."

The world waits.

Chapter 14
Even Superman Had Problems

It was in a small coal-mining community that overlooked a vast network of railroad tracks that Mother tried to raise three boys. Rural West Virginia lends itself to the scenic and serene, a Costa Rica without an ocean, but scenic settings don't inoculate one against dysfunctional behaviors that are developed as a defense against childhood pain and hurt.

We were a complete family unit throughout my adolescent years, but when childhood is exposed to infidelity and disharmony, one begins to question the value of "staying together for the children." The betrayal that my life was exposed to led to a sense of shame and guilt. My troubled heart's prescription was a quick burial for any and all painful events. The strangest thing about the Peatross family was that when bad things happened, nobody ever talked about them. So memories were repressed, and now I live with the pain of a lost childhood.

Granted, all people have problems. The only ones I know who don't have problems are those who have died. But let the normal developmental crisis years of a teenager be disturbed by parental infidelity, and childhood problems are compounded. That nice, healthy, little kid who was so comfortable with his peers and parents, who was so unconcerned about his looks, and whose awareness was completely outside of himself, all of a sudden seems like an alien. Parents who exacerbate a child's maturing process with their own dysfunction only delay the emotional development of a young man trying to become an adult.

My father was absent when I needed him at home with me. The memory of my dad crying on the stairway is so vivid that it seems as though it was only yesterday. I'll never forget my short stairway conversation with him. "Dad, why are you crying?" "Because your mother wants a divorce." I was traumatized like the millions of other teenagers who are raised in single parent family. Thoughts ran through my immature mind. "What did I do? How can I mend this problem? What if dad leaves and never comes back? What's mother doing in her room? Is she getting ready to take us all away?" This is agonizing self-talk for a teenager who is having his own personal crisis and who now has the problem of trying to fix his family.

I longed for my father. I needed him to teach me how to do the "man" things that I would soon be responsible for. I needed him to show me how to throw a ball, how to balance a checkbook, and how to love a wife. I needed his time and attention. But I had no control of the circumstances. Consequently, I entered adulthood unprepared and ill-equipped for life. Today, decades later, I am convinced that my off-centeredness is due to the absence of a father's mentoring during my critical developmental years. The sad part is that those I love the most today suffer the consequences of my early molding.

It was my mother who "stayed" with me through the teenage years. She managed to feed, to pay the bills, and to help three boys on less than $200 a month. She provided in every way, with the exception of introducing us to Jesus. Although, she did make one attempt at the spiritual when she delivered us to the front steps of a Methodist church, drove away, and later returned to pick us up. We were afraid to tell her about the preacher who rebuked us for disrupting the congregation during his sermon.

But there is a second act to my story. It began at a small university where God sent an angel into my life. God's like that you know: He writes other characters into our stories. In my case it was my wife. We soon fell in love and the rest is history. But there's one important footnote you should know about. She came from a Christian family. She introduced me to the Best Actor in my life story; Jesus. But of course, she's the best Supporting Actor and has been from the day I met her.

Does God have a plan for you? You bet He does! Psalm 139 tells us that while we were still inside our mother's wombs, God planned every step for us. His plan weaves its way through our lives from embryonic development to death. Maybe yours is a life that needed love, like mine. Maybe your marriage was a thing of beauty but now it's a tragic failure.

The great Scottish preacher Alexander McClaren said, "Be kind to everyone you meet because everyone you meet is fighting a battle." The only normal people I know are the folks I don't know well. Even Superman was dogged by kryptonite for half a century.

It's time to stop window-shopping for somebody else's life and live with our own inventory. God gives us all a special field to till and accept. If the soil is thinner, the rocks more numerous, and the prospects smaller, then so be it. That's how life is. So stop looking over the fence and daydreaming about what you could do with somebody else's field.

The real test isn't what you can do with somebody else's circumstances. The real test is what you can do with what you've been given, and in Jesus Christ we have been given much.

**Chapter 15
The Wilderness**

My legs trembled as I climbed a narrow stairway on a warm September evening. I had completed a series of studies from the scriptures and had made the decision to give my life to Jesus. My wife and two daughters stood at the bottom of the stairway and watched with anticipation as I disappeared into a small dressing room. The room was dimly lit and painted a schoolroom green. I walked past a full-length mirror and noticed what looked like a white jump suit hanging on the wall. The preacher smiled and said, "Don't worry, the baptismal robes will fit. No one's too tall, too small, or too thick to be fitted." My stomach began to cramp as I put one leg in the baptismal gown. Every emotion I've ever experienced was sandwiched in between my fear of giving my life to Christ and the peace that would follow my decision. I was on the verge of completing the biggest decision I would ever make. It was evident that Satan wanted me to reconsider.

As I toweled off, I felt relieved about the forgiveness that God had extended to me. After years of resistance, I had finally resigned as the manager of my own little world, and now I was about to embark on a new journey with a new Master. But I never considered the drastic changes that would have to take place over the next few months.

Only time has separated the similarities of my decision from the decisions the first-century "Jews-converted-to-Jesus" had to make. Like them, I carried over the remnants of a former life. Their comfort was found in circumcision; mine was found in the brown dried flower tops of marijuana. It was only a matter of weeks before I put my pot habit to death and buried it forever.

As time went on, I became serious about my commitment. My studies became more intensive. I was beginning to feel good about my progress. Those I admired and looked to began telling me that I was learning at an accelerated rate. My pride was now being fed by the "knowledge delusion." Now don't misunderstand me, Bible knowledge is good, but I had gradually begun to focus less and less on Jesus and more and more on doctrine. I was convinced that I was in the right church with the right theology, and anyone else outside of my little circle was doomed to an eternity without God.

For the next few years, God worked through people and circumstances to teach me of my misplaced emphasis. Try as I might, I realized that I couldn't find Jesus by trusting in myself. My academic prowess had only lead to a proud appreciation of my knowledge. I had invested all my early years in the *positions of scripture* and ignored the *Person of scripture.* Both humility and a passionate appreciation of Christ were missing. I had developed an orthodoxy that was crushing my life.

The Key To A Faithful Wilderness Experience

I knew that I couldn't survive life outside the Garden unless I developed an intimate relationship with God. Intimacy was something I had never experienced. It was frightening. But the battle raging in my soul was greater than my fear. I knew I couldn't overcome without Him. I had two choices, either continue on the present course and deny the pain or acknowledge my pain and use it as an opportunity to reach out into new areas of faith. I didn't find the former option a viable one, so I turned to the scriptures once again, only this time in an attempt to find Jesus.

When we find ourselves in the wilderness, we can only pray that our misdirected wandering will become a time of strengthening.

The Wilderness

Mark says that immediately after Jesus was baptized the Spirit *sent* (NIV), *impelled* (NAS), *drove* (RSV) Him into the wilderness (Mark 1:12-13). The word "sent" is a strong word that is used eleven times in Mark's writings. Each time he is describing the casting out of a demon.

Jesus didn't spend time basking in the glory of the heavenly voice, but He was immediately thrust into the Devil's wilderness. Heaven had opened and the Spirit descended; now Hell opened and Jesus was the playing field.

Likewise, we're sent from our conversion experience to the wilderness. There are hurdles to jump and battles to fight. No one is exempt from the wilderness of this world. It's a passageway to the Promise Land, but there are dangers inherent in the wilderness. Need I remind you what happened to Israel when they came out of Egypt? They left full of hope and faith in God, but in the short distance to the Promise Land, they stopped putting their hope and trust in God and instead trusted in themselves.

The key to a faithful wilderness experience is to remember the great commandment to "love God with all your heart, mind and soul." I must confess that telling me to love while wandering in the wilderness is like being commanded to be well when you're sick, to sing with joy when you're dying, and to run when your legs are broken. But this remains the first and great commandment, even in the wilderness. It's an open secret; love God —*even in the wilderness.*

Chapter 16
Anatomy of a Cardboard Life

Lassie. That name probably reminds you of a famous dog, but it's my little reminder that when we lie about what we have, who we know, or what we've done, we are simply propping up a vain life. Indeed it's *"better to be poor than a liar"* (Proverbs 19:22).

Years ago when I was in the first grade, I wanted so much to impress my friends and teachers that I would carry a picture of a collie in my back pocket. When the urge to get attention struck me, I would pull the crumpled picture out and say with a note of pride, "Here's my dog." It didn't matter that I was six-years old and it was 1955 and the date on the back of the picture said 1942. Old Lassie provided a convenient prop. That picture helped me become something I wasn't—and that is the essence of a shabby life.

Now, I am not sure how "shabby" a first-grader's life can be. I imagine all of us can point back to a time of immaturity and hopefully grin and thank the Lord that we've put away such childish things. Yet there are the "forever" immature, whom the Hebrew writer referred to as infants, that never become acquainted with righteousness. Truth telling requires vigilance on our part. Each of us must guard against the tendency to think there's a distinction between "big" and "little" or "white" and "black" lies.

Knowing how God views the sin of lying, I wonder why anyone would practice the deception of lying, even a "little white" one. The fact is that carefully planting a "little lie" here and there is easier than building a quality life. Lies are magnificent substitutes for the lazy man because building real character is hard work. It's far easier to pretend and let the lies provide the needed "props" for a cardboard life, a life lived as if everything consists of what you have or what you know or what you've done. It finds its happiness in leading others to believe they have things they don't have, know people they don't know, and have done things they have never done.

Tattered lives are as much a part of the story of God's dealings with man as are the quality lives of Abraham and Elijah, Cornelius and Paul. The shabby lives of Saul, Esau, Judas, and the Rich Young Ruler fill out the human drama. The classic illustration is the case of Ananias and Sapphira (Acts 5). Because they wanted to impress the apostles with their generosity after seeing what others had done (Acts 4:36-37), they told, what many today would consider, a "half-truth." Of course, it didn't work, and their cardboard lives came to an abrupt end—they had told their last "little lie."

How can we avoid the same failures? The only answer is to stay totally centered in Jesus and honor him with lives of honesty and integrity. It may mean saying, "I can't afford it," or "No, I've never met him," or "No, I've never done that." People of integrity know that truth isn't elastic and that half of the truth is no truth. Motive is the issue—there's a big difference between owning a license plate frame which says, "My other car is a Lexus," because you want people to believe you have one and doing it as a joke. The former is dressed to the hilt in "shabbiness." "Buy the truth and don't sell it" (Proverbs 23:23) isn't only a rule about sound doctrine but a rule for quality living as well.

Just what is this "quality life"? Perhaps it can be best described by making a spiritual adaptation to our previous definition of the "shabby life." That is, a life becomes quality when it is based upon *what you have* (forgiveness of sin), *who you know* (Jesus), *and what you're attempting* (to overcoming the evil one).

I think I'll throw my Lassie picture away.

Chapter 17
Jesus the Scorekeeper

As a child, my one obsession was baseball. My father was an avid baseball fan, and I can only assume that he passed the addiction on to me. From early spring to mid-October, it was part of the air we breathed. Whatever we did during the week, the voice of Joe Nuxhall reporting a Reds game was part of it. Even today, when I hear the sounds of a baseball game on the radio, I have strong tendency to want to stop everything I am doing.

There's just something about baseball that is different from all the other games. All it takes is a childhood of growing up with league standings and batting averages for it to get into your blood. Once you agonize through a pennant race with a team, you never recover. What I learned is that baseball is a dramatic presentation of some of life's most important and universal lessons.

I'm not saying that Abner Doubleday intended to make a theological statement on the meaning of life when he invented the game of baseball, but he did invent a game that dramatizes the human predicament of trying, but failing, to measure up to a standard of perfection.

The apostle Paul mentioned on more than one occasion a standard of perfection where achievement is impossible. As a matter of fact, he called the law's standard a "curse"(Galatians 3:13). It was a curse in the sense that it taught us of our sin and inability to live up to its standard. Not one of us is good enough, for we "*all have sinned and fallen short of the glory of God*"(Romans 3:21-26).

Measuring up to a Perfect Standard

Baseball is a game of measuring things against impossible standards. Everything is added up and kept as a statistic. Check next Sunday's newspaper, and you will find hundreds of numbers for different players and teams: team won-lost records, batting averages, RBI's, ERA's, and fielding percentages compared against every other team and player in the league.

A player's batting average is made public when it's printed in the paper and announced on television and radio. It's flashed in bright lights on the stadium scoreboard, even carried out to the three decimal points. Nobody says, "He's hitting pretty good." They say, "He's batting .295." Very precise measurements. There's no way to pretend success or hide failure. The numbers are recorded as statistics and become public information for the world to see.

The interesting thing about all this is that nobody does very well. The best hitters get about three hits in every ten tries. That's not a very good percentage for most jobs, but if you get three out of ten in baseball, management pays you a multi-million dollar salary. Be consistent and build your career on three out of ten, and you might be honored with a place in the Hall of Fame.

As I was growing up, my favorite team was the Cincinnati Reds, but my favorite player was a New York Yankee, Mickey Mantle. He hit some of the longest home runs I've ever seen, yet Mickey Mantle struck out 1,710 times in his career. That's a large number, yet he's one of the greatest stars the game has ever seen.

In fact, no one is very good when measure against the absolute batting average of 1000. That's an impossible standard that all players fall short of while the whole world watches. No one has even come halfway to perfection over the course of a season. All have fallen short.

The apostle Paul would appreciate the similarities in the batting average standard and the inability of the best Christian to come near the law's perfect standard of perfection. Baseball is a hard, judging master of all who set out to play the game, and life is a lot like that.

Luckily, there's another side of baseball, a side that is more giving and grace oriented. It's a side that allows everyone a chance to bat. It's a side that gives everyone the same number of balls, strikes, and outs. What makes baseball fairer than all the other games we watch and play is that it doesn't have a clock. (Maybe this makes the game fairer than life itself.) Unless it rains, everyone is allowed the same number of innings. Play doesn't stop until there is a winner and a loser. As that great baseball theologian, Yogi Berra, said, "It ain't over till it's over."

But maybe the best quality of the game is that it has the magic of the unexpected. There's always time for redemption.

If you're a baseball addict as I am, maybe you will remember the story of Bob Brenley. In 1986, Bob Brenley was the third baseman for the San Francisco Giants. In the fourth inning of a game against the Atlanta Braves, Brenley made an error on a routine ground ball. Four batters later he kicked another grounder. Then while he was scrambling after the ball, he threw wildly past home plate allowing a runner to score and the others to move up an extra base. Two errors on one play. A few minutes later, he muffed yet another play to become the first player in the twentieth century to make four errors in one inning.

Those of us who have made very public errors in one situation or another can empathize with what Bob Brenley must have felt as he walked off the baseball diamond that day in 1986, but in the very next inning, magic made its appearance when Bob Brenley stepped to the plate and hit a home run. In the seventh inning he came to bat again and hit a bases-loaded single, driving in two runs and tying the game. Then in the ninth inning with two outs and the game tied, Brenley hit a home run to win the game. His scorecard for the day read, three hits in five at bat, two home runs, four errors, four runs allowed, four runs driven in, including the game-winning run.

A mixture of hits and errors...sounds a little like my life. Brenley needed the second chance of grace. Don't we all? It's a certainty that grace won't erase your errors, but it gives you a chance to make up for them. When you're on God's team, it doesn't matter if you're only batting .200 because when you're weak, He is strong.

Besides, you're in good company. When Jesus lived here, He spent most of his time with the people who went 0 for 4 and muffed opportunity after opportunity with error after error. I think we've labeled them as "losers." I am glad Jesus doesn't judge as we do, aren't you?

The simple truth is that we all make errors, some of us more than others, but with Christ we're given the opportunity for a comeback. God's love is always seeking us, always following us, always overlooking the errors and giving us still another inning, still another chance at bat.

In Jesus, the scorekeeper cancels the errors and gives the losers another chance because with God, it ain't over till it's over.

Chapter 18
You Can't Understand

It left an indelible mark on my mind. I was standing three deep in a line at the water fountain between the gymnasium and the cafeteria when a home economics teacher pushed open the classroom door and announced the assassination of President John F. Kennedy. I don't recall her name, just the distressed look on her face.

A few years ago I was reminded of that day in Dallas, Texas, when the Prime Minister of Israel, Yitzhak Rabin, was assassinated. As I watched the evening news, the camera panned to an angry Israeli citizen who said, "These are the kinds of things that happen in America, not Israel." My initial thought was, "Yea, right. You're just plain wrong; these tragedies transverse every corner of this sin-damaged planet." Not long ago, two suicide terrorists in Yemen blew a hole in the side of the USS Cole that killed fifteen sailors. In that same newspaper, I read about a car bomb that exploded killing six people and about a mother from New York who tortured her six-year old child.

There's not a sensible person alive who hasn't felt compassion for the victims of such violence. When you contemplate a world where women are raped, children are abused, and wives live in fear of their husbands, it makes it difficult to envision the tranquil spirit that existed before sin in the Garden of Eden. Today we live in a world that is the antithesis of tranquility, a world gone mad.

Isaiah said, *"The wolf will live with the lamb, the leopard will lie down with the goat, the calf and the lion and the yearlings together; and a little child will lead them. The cow will feed with the bear, their young will lie down together, and the lion will eat straw like the ox. The infant will play near the hole of the cobra, and the young child put his hand in the viper's nest"* (Isaiah 11:6-9). Passages such as this one make me long for a creation where all of God's creatures live in a peace. If God wanted, He could snap His fingers and have wolves living peacefully with lambs and children harmlessly playing with cobras. Although it's most likely that this text symbolizes the peace a Christian experiences when he submits his life to the reign of Christ, it doesn't negate the desire for the return to a time when all of God's creation coexisted in a peaceful environment, a time when human dominion was so simple that a child could lead.[xvi]

The Peace of God

Maybe you're thinking of how desirable a utopian world would be, but this wasn't the idea Paul had in mind when he wrote a letter to a troubled church at Philippi (Philippians 4:1-9).

"...and the peace of God, which transcends all understanding will guard your heart and your mind in Christ Jesus" (Philippians 4:7).

The peace Paul promises is a peace that is achieved one person at a time. Once an individual receives this peace, God begins His work of guarding the heart and the mind. The image is that of a city being protected as a Roman garrison stands guard. Tradition says that when Paul was incarcerated, he was chained to a Roman solider who guarded him day and night. Equating a soldier's guarding with God's peace led J.B. Lightfoot to call this passage a verbal paradox. This is the only occasion in the New Testament where you find the expression "the peace of God." More than the peace God gives is the peace that God *is*. God gives and Christians receive.

This peace can't be put in a box, defined, or filed. It's a mystery beyond man's ability to comprehend or fully explain. Some have defined peace as the "cessation of fighting," but that's not a definition, rather a result. The peace of God is something we accept by faith, experience by grace, but never figure out by logic. Although we can't fully comprehend this peace, Paul says it still protects our heart and mind, even in the midst of conflict and danger. Even when the blessings of Christianity go beyond our grasp, the means of achieving the blessing is always simple and easy to understand.

Keys to Peace

The first key to peace is to rejoice in the Lord always (Phil.4:4). It seems strange that we would be commanded to do something that, on first appearance, seems to be a natural response to something good happening in our life, but not all the events of life are happy. When Paul wrote this epistle, he didn't write it from a Florida beach but from a Roman prison where he patiently awaited his pending trial before Nero Caesar. Chained to a guard, Paul puts pen to paper and writes, "rejoice." I am certain Paul had days when his concern blitzed his happiness, but Paul understood that there was a vast difference between happiness and joy. Happiness is "circumstance" dependent, while joy transcends circumstances. No matter what may be going on in this world, we can rejoice "in the Lord." Our sins have been forgiven; we have a Father in heaven who loves us, a big brother who died for us, and the Holy Spirit who intercedes for us. We're a forgiven family with a precious hope.

The second key to peace is to *"let your gentleness be evident to all"* (Phil. 4:5). The word *gentle* is from a Greek word that means *strength under control.* The image that Paul paints for us is that of a wild stallion being brought under the reins of control yet continuing to retain its power. The result is a tame and gentle stallion whose power is now managed and controlled by its master. I like Chuck Swindoll's definition of gentleness. He calls it a "sweet reasonableness." Gentleness is a managed attitude that makes the decision to relax, no matter the moment, because God has the controls. It's when we allow God authority over our life that we'll develop a forbearing spirit toward our family and friends. It's been almost two decades since I resigned as the manager of my little universe, but I still must die daily and recommit myself to the reins of God's control.

Chapter 19
Musings on Human Tragedies

In his spiritual autobiography, William Barclay, the Scottish scholar, writes of the tragedy he experienced when he lost his twenty-one year old daughter and son-in-law in a boating accident. He writes, "God did not stop that accident at sea, but He did still the storm in my own heart so that somehow my wife and I came through that terrible time."

Some time later, Barclay received an anonymous letter regarding his daughter's death. It said, "I know why God killed your daughter. It was to save her from the corruption of your heresies." Barclay said that if he had known the writer's address, he would have written back in pity, not anger, saying as John Wesley did, "Your God is my devil."

This story clearly illustrates the differences in the way one sees God. Both Barclay and the anonymous letter writer laid the blame squarely at God's feet. Barclay implies that God chose not to, but could have stopped his daughter's accident at sea. The letter writer expressed his belief that God tipped the boat over and killed the young couple.

Those who have experienced the pain of losing a child, as Barclay did, can understand the fear one feels when there is no good reason for the loss. It's only natural to want to hold God responsible in some way.

Lewis Smedes, in his book *Forgive and Forget*, retells an old story about a tailor who has just exited the synagogue and meets a rabbi outside the entrance door.

"Well, what have you been doing in the synagogue, Lieb Astrom?" the rabbi asks.

"I was saying prayers, Rabbi."

"Fine, and did you confess all your sins, even your *little* sins?"

"Yes, I confessed that I sometimes cut my cloth on the short side. I cheat on a yard of wool by a couple of inches."

"You said that to God, Lieb Astrom?"

"Yes, Rabbi, and more." I said, "Lord, I cheat on pieces of cloth. You let little babies die, but I am going to make you a deal. You forgive me of my little sins, and I'll forgive you of the big ones."

While I don't agree with the tailor's theology, I have to believe that this was the best the tailor had to offer in dealing with the pain of his tragedy. There was one thing the tailor and Barclay had in common. They both held God accountable.

When a tragedy invades a person's life and the pain turns to blame, God willingly welcomes our anguished approach. He understands because His Son experienced the tragedy of the cross. God sees any crisis as an opportunity to develop a deeper relationship with the person. There are those rare occasions where God chooses to intervene and circumvent a tragedy, but if one is going to grow and develop a greater dependence on God, he must remember that this is the exception and not the rule.

Tragic accidents come with the territory of freedom. Barclay understood that God could have prevented his daughter's boat from over turning that day, but instead of continuing to blame God, he made the decision to accept the crisis and the pain that went with it. The result was a deeper relationship with his creator.

Jesus And Tragedy

It was shortly after a cohort of Roman soldiers, who were known for their barbaric atrocities, had brutally murdered innocent men, women, and children that Jesus challenges the crowd with this tragic headliner out of Jerusalem: *"Do you think these were deserving of such brutality? Do you think they were worse sinners than all the rest who met in the temple that day? I tell you the truth. The same thing could happen to you. Be spiritually prepared and repent"* (Luke 13:1-5).

"Do you think those eighteen construction workers who were crushed to death by the Tower of Siloam were worse sinners than the other construction workers who were on the same construction site that day? Not at all. The truth is the same thing could happen to you. Turn to God before it's too late" (Luke 13:4).

Sometimes there's no explanation for the bad things that happen to people. That's an answer that doesn't sit well with our penchant for blame. Surely, someone must be liable for the collapse of the Tower of Siloam. Surely, someone must be to blame for the boating accident. Someone must have been drinking. They should have checked the weather. Maybe they weren't qualified as boaters. God please give us the information so we can know whom to blame.

The challenge for those of us who call ourselves Christians is not to look for someone to blame but to take the postscripts from the above stories and make them our first thoughts when tragedy visits our lives or the lives of those we know. "Were they spiritually prepared?"

Chapter 20
Trust

After God appeared to Job in a whirlwind (after he lost his possessions, family, and health), Job made some penetrating observations about the ostrich:

> *The wings of an ostrich flap joyfully,*
> *But they cannot compare with the*
> *pinions and feathers of the stork. She*
> *lays her eggs on the ground and lets*
> *them warm in the sand, unmindful*
> *that a foot may crush them. She*
> *treats her young harshly, as if they*
> *were not hers: she cares not that her*
> *labor was in vain, for God did not*
> *endow her with wisdom or give*
> *her a share of good sense.*
> *Yet when she spreads her feathers to run,*
> *she laughs at horse and rider*
> (Job 39:13-18).

How often have we heard that an ostrich buries her head in the sand? In reality she doesn't; if she did, she would smother. Yet you and I may imitate this strange bird in a variety of ways.

Do we act as though life doesn't count, think that we can build our "nest" anywhere we please without being disturbed? Do we sometimes give the impression we don't care how our children are raised? Could someone point a finger at us and say, "God didn't endow you with wisdom or good sense?"

Often we hide from the world by burying our head in the sand, ignoring everything except our own personal needs. This self-centeredness leads us to believe that we can make it without

God. As we whiz by in life, we shout out to anyone listening, "So far, so good!" What happens then when we run headlong into a barricade, when we lose our job due to "downsizing," when our teenager daughter must live with an unwanted pregnancy, when our spouse informs us that he or she is going in a separate direction, or when we lose a parent to Alzheimer's? What then?

J.B. Phillips, the author of *The New Testament in Modern English,* called Jesus' beatitudes in Matthew 5:3-9 the "recipe for happiness," yet he vividly painted the contrast of Jesus' words by rewriting the beatitudes in the way most people think they should read:

Blessed are the "pushers": for they get on in the world.
Blessed are the hard-boiled: for they never let life hurt them.
Blessed are they who complain: for they get their own way
in the world.
Blessed are the blasé: for they never worry over their sins.
Blessed are the slave drivers: for they get results.
Blessed are the knowledgeable men of the world: for they know
their own way around.
Blessed are the troublemakers: for they make people take
notice of them.

Jesus, however, began His beatitudes, *"Blessed are those who know their need of God, for to them belongs the kingdom of heaven."* The question we must ask is, "Do we realize we have this need?"

"As the deer pants for streams of water, so my soul pants for you, O God. My soul thirsts for God, for the living God" (Psalm 42:1-2). Call it spiritual hunger, but it's still there in all of us. We get thirsty for satisfying water, and it's always available.

Henri Nouwen says the real question of life is, "Do you know the incarnate God?" He explains, "In our world of loneliness and despair, there's an enormous need for men and women who know God, a heart that forgives, that cares, that reaches out and wants to heal." Then he adds this insightful line, "It's a heart that wants only to give love and receive love in response."[xvii]

You can remain as the dumb ostrich when it comes to your heart's response to God and His Son or you can submit your heart to His heart in loving faith. You will then receive the gift of His approval. In the words of songwriter Thomas O. Chisholm:

> Bring Christ your broken life,
> So marred by sin.
> He will create anew,
> Make whole again;
> Your empty, wasted years,
> He will restore,
> And your iniquities,
> Remember no more.

Chapter 21
The Truth About Us

It's probable that someone reading these words is fighting an inner battle with a ghost from the past. The skeleton in one of yesterday's closets is beginning to rattle louder and louder. Putting adhesive tape around the closet door does little to muffle the chattering bones. You wonder, "Who knows?"

The anchor that tumbled off your boat is dragging and snagging on the bottom. Guilt and anxiety have come aboard, pointing out the great, dark hulks of the shipwreck below. They drill "worry holes" in your hull, and you're beginning to sink.

It may be true that you've done things that would embarrass you if they became public knowledge. Maybe you've committed a tragic sin that was never traced back to you. You may have a criminal record or a moral change or a domestic conflict that, to this moment, is private information. Your memories are covered by the sands of time and you feel that if they come to light, they'll cripple your reputation.

Before you surrender your case as hopeless, consider the liberating evidence offered in the pages of the Bible. You can read story after story of men and women whom God used in spite of their past. Abraham, founder of Israel and labeled "the friend of God," was once a worshipper of idols. Joseph had a prison record; on one occasion when the heat was turned up he lied, yet he became prime minister of Egypt. Moses was a murderer but later became the one who delivered his nation from the slavery of Pharaoh. Jephthah was an illegitimate child who ran around with a tough bunch of hoods before he was chosen by God to become His personal representative. Rahab was a harlot in the streets of Jericho but was later used in such a mighty way that God enlisted her among the members of His hall of fame in Hebrews 11.

Still unconvinced? There's more. Eli and Samuel were both poor, inconsistent fathers; however, they proved to be strong men of God. Jonah and John Mark were missionaries who cowardly ran away from hardship but became profitable later. Peter openly denied the Lord and cursed Him, only to return and become one of God's best spokesmen among the early infant church. Paul was so hard and vicious in his early life the disciples and apostles refused to believe he had actually become a Christian. The files of heaven are filled with stories of redeemed, refitted renegades and rebels.

There's not a single Christian who is free from "shameful things." The ones who think otherwise are worse than all the rest combined. We were all taken from the same dunghill. We all fight the same fight with the same filth of the flesh regardless of how beautifully we sing, how piously we pray, or how wonderfully we teach from a text in the Bible.

Mark it down, when God forgives, He forgets. He's not only willing but pleased to use any person, just as long as he or she is clean today. You may be a cracked or chipped vessel or you may have never been used before. Count on this—this past ended one second ago. From this point onward, you can be used in many different ways for His honor so throw the guilt and anxiety overboard...draw the anchor...trim the sails...man the rudder...a strong gale is coming!

Chapter 22
Parable of a Lobster

Years ago, when Kroger first began stocking their stores with lobster, I would stand in front of the glass case and watch with fascination.

Lobsters have those dreaded pincers. One pincer is made for crushing; it's shorter, hard, and viselike. The other pincer is long and serrated, made for cutting and tearing. Lobsters have hard, tough shell, on the outside and powerful tails that propels them away from danger.

Many of us are like lobsters in the way we relate to one another. We develop a hard shell for protection, and on rare occasions we attack by cutting and crushing. Often when relationships begin to get too close, we run and hide.

The hard shell on the lobster was put there to protect his jelly-like insides. Unlike the lobster, we're soft on the outside (because our toughness is on the inside). We have a hard skeletal internal structure, muscle for strength and action, but on the outside, we have skin that's sensitive to the touch.

We're made to touch and be touched. No other living creature was made to enjoy such closeness as found in a relationship. Humans are uniquely created for embracing. On the day that we're born, we need another human's touch. On the last day of our life, we're still in need of a human's touch. The real question comes in between those two days. How are you going to find the courage to be close to another human being?

Why are we so protective? Maybe part of the reason is we haven't discovered that loving by its very nature includes pain.

Hemingway expressed it in a profound way: "Life breaks everyone and afterwards some are strong in the broken places." Being close to another human being requires brokenness. What is brokenness in a relationship?

Brokenness is the realization that you're not always right, that you say and do some incredibly hurtful things, but having the courage to let the impact of your wrongs register in your heart. Do you feel and accept the wounds, or do your defenses go up? Brokenness is allowing yourself to become more open and vulnerable. It's allowing transparency to be a part of your way. It's accepting who you are but dealing with the parts of you that are in need of change. This is humbling but powerful.

The psalmist recognized the redeeming power of being broken: *"Let me hear joy and gladness; let the bones you have crushed rejoice"* (Psalm 51:8).

The strength that follows brokenness equips you to handle the rages of life. It makes you more resilient and less rigid. Rigidity only prepares you for a greater shattering; it has no flexibility.

Relationships break everyone. If you approach relationships like a lobster with a hard shell, then one hard blow will shatter you. That's the peril of the lobster, and that will be your peril as well. The choice is between being broken and being shattered. You make that choice in every important relationship.

If you choose being broken over being shattered, it will open the way for a more powerful closeness in your relationships and will protect you from the fatal relationship blows. It will make you strong in the broken places.

Mary had a brokenness that gave her a courageous heart. Yes, her heart had been broken many times. But shattered? Never. She would emerge strong enough to be there for her son, even at the foot of his cross. She knew how to handle the blows of life.

When you learn brokenness, you'll be able to find the most incredible closeness a human can know.

Chapter 23
Fear, Doubt and an Empty Tomb

The early disciples were comfortable with Jesus' humanity. What I have struggled with on numerous occasions, they readily accepted. They had come to know Him as you and I come to know any man. They walked with Him, touched Him, saw Him hungry, tired, and distressed. They were working with a visual image, a sensory perception. To them He was as real as you or I. This would later be the source of their disbelief and defeatism as they huddled together in an upper room after His death. To them, the death of a man marks the end of his dreams, his leadership, and his power. It wasn't Jesus' humanness, but His divinity that they struggled with.

It's true that Peter made a magnificent confession on behalf of the disciples, saying, *"You are the Christ, the Son of the living God,"* but it's obvious that they didn't grasp the meaning or the magnitude of their confession. Judging from their responses to Jesus, I believe it's fair to say that they saw Jesus only as a man of God, a worker of miracles, a dearly loved companion, a brilliant teacher, an irreproachable leader; but He was a man, like them, who would suffer the fate that would befall all men. When Jesus died, it was a demoralizing blow for the disciples. Their despair was like that of a loyal subject who had lost their king. It wasn't as if Jesus had never spoken of his death and resurrection; they simply had, somehow, failed to hear.

Faced with the empty tomb, the disciples' disbelief rivaled that of the enemy's. When Mary told the disciples that she had seen Jesus alive, they didn't believe her. Luke writes that the reports of the women seemed "like nonsense" to the disciples. They weren't easily persuaded. The incredulity of the disciples is of powerful, apologetic significance. It's not that they didn't believe the resurrection story, but they were filled with such despair at His passing. This gives great weight to their final testimony of the fact of His resurrection.

The enemies of Jesus add fuel to the apologetic fires, taking such precautions against the theft of His body that they unwittingly engineer a setting that will provide evidence of the highest veracity. I have always believed that the most convincing proof of the resurrection of the Lord is the silence of His enemies. All they had to do was to produce the body, and the foolish heresy would have ended for all time. Having strategically prepared themselves, they were fully aware of the consequences. They went to Pilate and said, *"Sir we remember that while he was still alive that deceiver said, 'After three days I will rise again.' So give the order for the tomb to be made secure until the third day. Otherwise, his disciples may come and steal the body and tell the people that he has been raised from the dead. This last deception will be worse than the first"* (Matthew 27:63-66). Pilate told them to go and make the tomb as secure as they knew how.

In the midst of all this fear and doubt, think of what proof it must have taken to bring skeptical Thomas to his knees, crying, *"My Lord and my God!"* It took nothing short of touching the resurrected body of Jesus. What was meant to be the end of a man declared Him to be the Son of God: His tomb is still there but by the power of God, it's empty. The story that burned in the hearts of men centuries ago continues to flame in the hearts of men today—and truly the chief priests and Pharisees were right when they predicted that an empty tomb wouldn't be the end but the beginning.

Chapter 24
God's Others—Thems and Theys

Recently, I glanced back at my high school annual. As I thumbed through the sports section, I noticed that surrounding the team picture was a group of action shots taken from the football games. One of the pictures was of a classmate trying to block a punt. Another picture was taken of a halfback running around the end for a big gain. I noticed that the bigger players, all linemen, were mostly lying on the ground as a result of those bone-crunching blocks they had placed on the opposition's linemen. (We forget that that their blocks spring those little halfbacks free.)

If my memory serves me right, it's these big kids that do most of the work but receive little of the credit. All the headlines and honors go to the running backs—the smaller faster guys that nobody can catch (but they had to get past those big guys on the other team first). Of course, this only happened if the bigger linemen on the offensive team blocked those other big guys on the opposite team.

Everybody loves recognition, yet honor is seldom a fair creature. We Christians are commanded to be lights in the world. Some Christians end up like those huge spotlights that announce mall openings and new movies, while others of us are more like the tiny little flashlights that you carry in your glove compartment. Some folks get all the credit, while others are barely noticed. We may as well admit it, some of us have to play on the line and let the running backs get the accolades.

Please don't misunderstand me. There are many in the kingdom deserving of recognition. I wouldn't want to detract from their accomplishments and sacrifices because their work is vital and their recognition is well-earned. The scriptures are replete with the names and deeds of men who have stood out in their service, and God has honored them by pointing to their examples: Abel, Enoch, Noah, Isaac, Jacob, Sarah, Joseph,

Moses, Rahab, Gideon, Barak, Samson, Jephthah, David, and Samuel. The eleventh chapter of Hebrews lauds these Christians for their faith and their feats. Why discredit someone whose light has shone brighter; why not give them well-deserved recognition?

Hebrews 11 also attests to the feats of the "others" (verse 35) and "they" (verse 37). Many Christians are included in that list. In fact, most of God's heroes will be seen upon this earth only as "they" or "them." All of these God knows, recognizes, and appreciates, but the honors will have to wait until we meet Him in heaven. Be certain that God knows the names and feats of the "unheralded Saints": the mothers who raise godly children without a father, the workers who endure ridicule on the job without retaliation, the God-chasers who wear the badge of love and grace while standing for the truth and refraining from the pressures of the legalist. He knows and recognizes those in difficult places as they continue to teach the gospel, the "little" congregations who are dedicated in their effort to teach and reach the lost, husbands and wives who love, children who honor, aged men and women who are not able to be in the assembly, widows who battle the loneliness every day, preachers, elders, deacons, teachers, and worship leaders who never hold seminars or meetings, who never oversee large congregations and never lead hundreds in thought or song. God knows.

Humans often fail to see those who are behind an effort. Every running back in the football Hall of Fame had at least five blockers, most of whom are long forgotten. We're inclined to honor those whose efforts are the most public and widespread. They're certainly worthy, but we need to remember that there are the "others," the "thems" and "theys," whose names just may also be in God's Hall of Fame.

Chapter 25
Extremophiles

Christians are "extremophiles" who perform remarkable acts of discipleship as they experience suffering, self-denial, and even loss of life.

You've never met this unique creature because it's a microorganism. You can't see it. The only place it lives is in environments where the temperature is at least 170 degrees Fahrenheit with an optimum temperature of over 215 degrees. (Water boils at 212.)

Its name is "Pyrococcus Furiosus." Let's do that again. First name: Py-ro-coc-cus. Last name: Fur-i-o-sus. Good!

Pyro is only one of many microorganisms attracting the attention of scientists today. Biotechnologists are learning a lot from organisms living way out there in dangerous places, on the edge. They call these microbes "extremophiles"—a name that literally means "extreme-lovers."

Extremophiles are microorganisms that thrive in hot springs, polar ice caps, salty lakes, and acidic fields—not the kinds of places you'd want to be vacationing this summer! They simply love to live in conditions that would kill humans and most of the plants and animals we have come to know. "Extremophile microbes are also busy industrialists," reports *The Futurist* magazine, "producing enzymes that are enormously useful in food, chemical, pharmaceutical, waste treatment and other industries."

Let's go back to our little friend Pyro. Let's say you need an enzyme. What you really need is an extremophile. So you contact a California biotech firm, which tells you that a bleaching enzyme produced by Pyro and some of his hyperthermophilic relatives (who are living in the scalding geothermal springs of Yellowstone National Park) could provide an alternative to chlorine in paper-whitening processes. Yellowstone's extreme environment also yields substances useful for making perfume, beer, and other commercial products (Cynthia G. Wagner, "Biotech Goes to Extremes," *The Futurist*, October 1998, 11).

We've heard of extremophiles before. Perhaps we just didn't realize it. From the beginning of the Old Testament to the book of Revelation, we are pointed to the "Greatest Extremophile of All Time."

In the district of Caesarea Philippi, Jesus reveals himself to be an extremophile, showing his disciples that *"he must go to Jerusalem and undergo great suffering at the hands of the elders and chief priests and scribes, and be killed, and on the third day be raised"* (Matthew 16:21). When Peter objects to this extremely painful prediction, Jesus turns and says, "Get behind me, Satan! ... you are setting your mind not on divine things but on human things." It seems that for Jesus, life on the edge is divine.

He then calls his disciples to join him in being one who lives in extreme environments. *"If any want to become my followers,"* says Jesus, *"let them deny themselves and take up their cross and follow me. For those who want to save their life will lose it, and those who lose their life for my sake will find it"* (Matthew 16:24-25).

Following the strange logic of extremophilic microbes, disciples are to do enormously useful work while living in environments that would kill most people. They are to experience suffering, self-denial, and even loss of life, but in the process, they will serve others and ultimately find their real selves. The divine irony of the gospel is that loss for Christ's sake leads to heavenly gain.

The benefits of being an extremophile are found on several levels. For starters, life in a challenging environment can make us stronger, wiser, and more secure in our convictions. It was no accident that the ancient Israelites got stronger through their period of oppression in Egypt. Exodus tells us that the Egyptians set taskmasters over them to oppress them with forced labor, and under the whip the Israelites built the cities of Pithom and Rameses for Pharaoh. *"But the more they were oppressed, the more they multiplied and spread, so that the Egyptians came to dread the Israelites"* (Exodus 1:12).

Remember it was Hemingway who said, "Sometimes life breaks us, but then we become stronger in the broken places." Sometimes challenges overwhelm us, but then we acquire wisdom that helps us to meet and overcome those challenges.

Sometimes we lose our faith in people and in the world around us, but then our faith in God becomes more secure.

We learn that every breath we take is a gift from our loving Lord and that the promises of God are more trustworthy than any promises made to us by bosses, teachers, family members, or friends.

An extremophile is not a person who disdains the world but is instead a person who discovers that the world does not contain salvation. Strength and wisdom and faith are always to be found on the edges of the world's comfort, in the challenging places where God resides. This is not to say that an extremophile is an extremist. Christians who live on the edge are not people who go looking for oppression or suffering or martyrdom.

For example, twenty-four-year-old Julia Butterfly Hill has spent a year living in a tree she calls Luna. This forest activist scurried up the boughs of the old-growth redwood in California to protest the logging practices of Pacific Lumber Company.

"People ask me what it will take for me to come down," she says. "I want to come down to a world where there is no more clear-cutting, no more herbicides sprayed on our trees, and the remaining three percent of our ancient forests are protected forever."

While we may admire Julia Hill for going to great lengths to take a stand for her beliefs – perching as a lightning rod 180 feet above ground in a giant redwood – many question the effectiveness of making ultimatums from extremist positions. Christian extremophiles take stands not in timber tops, but at timberline – in the rough-and-tumble engagements with other people where life is harsh and difficult.

It is where people live, in the marginal and transitional worlds of Egyptians and Israelites, blacks and whites, rich and poor, GenXers and retirees, that extremophiles take their stand. It's in the midst of real-life joys and pains that they lose their lives for the sake of Christ, and it is in this process that they discover a life radically real and extremely worthwhile. Extremophiles are disciples who are

- Extremely compassionate: willing to visit the infected sick in hospitals, the incontinent elderly in nursing homes, and the immune- deficient AIDS patients in hospices.

- Extremely humble: able to see that every good gift comes from God alone and that personal talents and resources should inspire gratitude, not pride.
- Extremely patient: committed to working with challenging children, adolescents with attitude, and young adults who are struggling with their faith.
- Extremely forgiving: willing to forgive not just once, or twice, but again and again because they know that God has forgiven them again and again.
- Extremely loving: volunteering to do Bible studies in prisons, visit and sing in retirement homes, and take dinners to the homeless shelters.
- Extremely faithful: living out a committed and trusting relationship with God, with spouse, with family members and friends, knowing that faithful living in an uncertain world is at the heart of a life that is real and worthwhile.

Extremophiles do all this enormously worthwhile work because it gives them great joy. It gives them a sense of satisfaction and a rush of pleasure that could never be found by punching a clock and drawing a paycheck. To make our activity look *good* for people is a challenge for us all, and it can be good if we take up our crosses with conviction and do the work of discipleship.

The call of Christ is to be extremophiles, not extremists: people who discover strength, wisdom, and faith in challenging environments and who find a rush of joy and satisfaction in being extremely compassionate, humble, patient, forgiving, loving, and faithful.

God has not promised us safety, but rather participation in an adventure called the Kingdom. That seems to me to be great news in a world that is literally dying of boredom.

The adventure called the Kingdom is an adventure for Pyro-Christians – people of God, who can warm things up, set the community on fire for Christ.

It is an extremophilic journey that challenges us to do enormously useful work while living in situations that would terrify most people, way out there, in dangerous places, on the edge.

It may involve suffering and self-denial, but in the process, it will enable us to serve others and ultimately find our real selves.

Such an extreme adventure will be threatening, challenging, thrilling, and satisfying – but never, ever boring.

Pyro-Christianus Furiosus!

Chapter 26
Death Before Resurrection

Much has been written about the "death of the church," at least in its more traditional form. There is certainly some degree of arrogance and exaggeration mixed in with these prophetic voices. However, the thing about these analysts is that they are generally telling the truth. Make no mistake; a revolution is under way. Postmodernism has grabbed our culture by the neck, and it isn't letting go. The winds of change are blowing, and if they continue, they may just blow the house down. Certainly the number of thinkers aware of these cultural quakes is growing. In fact, it is becoming trendy to talk of "postmodernism," and the small circle of reformers isn't that small any more. This "inner circle" even faces the possible danger of eventually being mistaken as an updated, goateed version of its earlier counterpart. Don't get me wrong. The power in the Christian subculture has by no means shifted, but it will. The day will eventually come when many of the charges being leveled at current church institutions will no longer be challenged—those charges, which deserve to be, will become accepted assumptions. In the meantime, there will be certain tensions between the reformers and the establishment. The current church and the coming church face rough waters, and it is my opinion that both sides must proactively embrace both grace and hope as we prepare for what will be.

For those of us recognizing the need for the church to engage the myriad issues postmodernism brings, we need to be aware that the process that will lead us to this inevitable outcome requires death. I hate to state the obvious, but here goes: death hurts. We may be so caught up in our passion for change that we callously brush past the emotional turmoil our brothers and sisters in Christ face. Many of those in preceding generations fought their own battles and waged their own wars. Their battle scars represent a cause they gave their life to, and it shouldn't be take lightly. It may be possible that a certain amount of their resistance to current trends may be that they are simply worn out. They are enjoying some of the rewards of a hard-fought life, and they don't cherish the idea of a new call to arms. This may be the appropriate time for another obvious fact that shouldn't need to be stated: we are answering the same battle cry. We may feel at times that we live in different worlds, but we belong to the same Kingdom. I think those of us who are passionate about incarnating the message of the Gospel to our culture, should, at times, pause long enough to make certain that we are also incarnating the grace of Christ to our brothers and sisters who have not come to the same conviction.

Another humble reminder is that every fresh movement brings with it a certain amount of extra baggage. At times we are blinded by the passion of the moment, and we do not clearly see that having a lot of it right does not make us immune to getting some of it wrong. It is interesting that our reaction to the modernistic tendency to categorize everything ad nauseam sometimes tempts us to neatly package up all the ones with whom we disagree as hopelessly modern. You know, what's good for the goose…

Wisdom tells us that we have much to learn from those who have walked the path before us. We need to listen to those with whom we disagree as much as we need to listen to those who share our positions; in fact, we may need to listen to them more. We may not always come to the same conclusions, but most criticisms offer some measure of truth. Besides, believe it or not, the time will come when our generation will be standard bearers for the status quo. To some degree, each generation's revolutionaries are the next generation's elder statesmen.

God has obviously placed a divine calling on the souls of a generation, a calling to boldly step into the future, unfettered by the chains of a powerful religious system insisting on conformity. As this saga lives itself out, the heart of God and the cause of the Kingdom would be best served by humble, courageous explorers who learn to balance an unswerving commitment to the call with an undying, respectful love for those who have gone before. If a season of death is required, it would seem that we should allow for a season of mourning as well.

The best part of God's stories is always the ending. Good triumphs over evil; wayward sons come home; death gives way to life. For those who are sensing the doom of the indictment of death upon much of the current church system, this is the way it must be. This is the way of hope. This is the way of life. The spiritual truth we must remember is that the promise of resurrection is hollow without the pain of death. When alluding to His own death and resurrection, Jesus reminded His followers that in order for there to be a bountiful harvest, a grain of wheat would have to fall to the ground and die so that new life could spring up.

The modern church has somehow grabbed a shortsighted view of God's promises to the church. God did say that the "church would prevail" and that we would be "more than conquerors," but I don't think that He necessarily had our particular version of Americanized Christianity as the focal point of His promise. The fear of death may be the result of our mistaken tendency to define the church by our own perceptions rather than allowing God's mind to shape our understanding. When we cling to our systems and categories more than we embrace the living, breathing truth of this community of faith where God's Spirit continually breathes new life, death may be the only remedy.

It challenges our sensibilities, but this is cause for celebration. The miracle of resurrection hinges on the reality of death. A Savior who resurrected from an afternoon nap would be meaningless, to say nothing of ridiculous. A church which resurrected from a difficult cultural war would be purposeless, to say nothing of ineffective. However, a Savior who resurrected from a bloody death on a wooden cross ignited a call to change the world. And after facing its own torturous death, the church can be resurrected to carry on this call once again. I am not suggesting that this will be a painless process, but I am suggesting that sometimes pain is the only way.

This death may take on numerous forms. It may be a crisis of faith, a total disorientation with long-held assumptions, a sense of deep regret, or a struggle between those preparing for a funeral and those still celebrating birthdays. Some churches will see death take its ultimate toll; they will cease to exist. For some churches, the truest, most hopeful gift they can offer the Kingdom is to die so that the Spirit can bring new life elsewhere.

Death is a constant plot in God's story. It is as old as the cross and an empty tomb. The question is not whether death will come, but whether or not we will bravely walk into the future with grace, embracing the reality of death and anticipating the hope of resurrection.

Chapter 27
Welcome to the X-treme Church

With falling attendance and a growing concern for the future, some churches have opted for the latest "marketing-blitz" in an attempt to attract a targeted audience. Challenged to overcome mediocrity, they have shaped a "new church" for a new generation. Unfortunately, they've sold out to anything that looks trendy in an effort to augment their declining attendance. They've created the *X-treme* church. Instead of remembering Jesus, the suffering servant, they rally around Jesus Christ Super Star. In this context, Jesus is not Jesus—but a symbol for the divine, a concept of the Holy. Church services transform into entertainment spectacles. The preacher is an entertainer, a comedian, and a deliverer of the weekly "warm fuzzy." The contribution is the price-of-admission. The church service is nothing more than a talent show.

Churches want to "become postmodern," because some keynote speaker told them it brings in the young people. What they create is a light show that is not post-anything, but hyper-modern. Sure some people buy it, but do they really get anything? Has the gospel just become another marketing scheme, another sell-job to a certain target audience of co-dependent people? Is the Church of Jesus Christ just good therapy for consumer-friendly America?

Moving to a new Edge: From Extreme to Authentic

Churches trying to *do* postmodernism are missing the point. Postmodernism is the context that a specific generation operates out of, not the goal. This generation wants what anyone else would desire, the possibility to connect with the holiness of God in a loving community of honest people with the same hopes; simply pursuing a postmodern paradigm cannot solve this. You can follow all the tactics, methods, and models, but if it does not connect people with the reality of

God, forget it! All you will have is community-in-a-can. This generation can see a sell-job from a mile away.

Ultimately, they don't want the X-treme; they want the authentic.

Tim Celek and Dieter Zander put it best in their book *Inside the Soul of a New Generation* (Zondervan Publishing):

Some churches that want to reach out to Busters (those born between 1965-1980) make an understandable error. Don't people who have been raised on VCRs and computers require a multimedia blitz to get their attention? Aren't dry-ice smoke, mirrors, strobes, and videos a must if you want to speak the Busters' language? Our answer and our experience is, in a word, 'no.' ...Busters do not want to be entertained, but they will not allow themselves to be bored (P.66).

Celek and Dieter believe (and I agree) this generation does not want to be entertained so much as they want to be engaged. They desire intimacy, high touch and low-tech experiences. These ideas, of course, are great in theory, but it is another thing altogether to apply them in the daily grind of ministry.

How easily we fall into the trap of ministry simulation!

Chapter 28
Reformation Through Team Ministry

Those who built on the wall, and those who carried burdens, loaded themselves so that with one hand they worked at construction, and with the other hand carried a weapon.

Every one of the builders had his sword girded at his side as he built. And the one who sounded the trumpet was beside me. Then I said to the nobles and rulers, and the rest of the people, "The work is great and extensive, and we are separated far from one another on the wall. Wherever you hear the sound of the trumpet, rally to us there. Our God will fight for us" (Nehemiah 4:17-19).

One of the astonishing things about Nehemiah Chapters 3-5 is that virtually *everyone* is involved in the work of rebuilding. There is no apparent distinction between leaders and people.

In fact, even Nehemiah and his servant worked together on the wall. Nehemiah himself did not take the portion of food that was rightly his as governor (5:15), but instead personally fed 150 at his table daily (5:17). In the process of working together, the people of God rediscovered community. Team ministry will be increasingly important in the new work that God is doing. No longer will authority be restricted by a few elders, creating huge bottlenecks in the work of building the Kingdom.

One day this fall I was out walking with my wife in the hills near our home. As is typical for a late fall day near a West Virginia lake, some Canadian geese were forming a huge V above the hillside, heading south. From our vantage point, we were almost at eye level with the formation. I watched with fascination as I saw something take place that I had only previously heard about. The lead goose dropped from the front of the V to the rear, and another goose took his place. I felt the Lord was providing an illustration of what His body should be. Leadership must be flexible and should be shared. Breaking the trail for the entire V formation is tiring. The lead goose bears the brunt of the forces in the air. Each goose along the V does less work than the goose in front. Eventually, the lead goose gets tired and trades his position with the next goose. This allows each goose time to rest and alternately to experience the exhilaration of being out in front. Geese seem to have no need for control and no lack of humility!

There are a number of challenges we face with true team ministry. First, leaders are accustomed to control. If God is in control, what are we to do? We thought that was our job. If just anyone can bring a message in our services, where does that leave our sermon? We are accustomed to being valued for our highly visible abilities. Will the church still need us? Our insecurities become not only our problem but also a bottleneck to ministry. We need to remind ourselves that our task is not to *do* the work, but to equip others to serve. We need to believe and practice Ephesians 4:16, which says the body is built "as each part does its work."

Second, professionalism has crept into our churches. "Let the professional do it." Both members and ministers are affected by this thinking. It's helpful to get outside our own culture for perspective. W.C. Lees, in *Second Thoughts on Missions*, writes,

"Let me picture for you a jungle friend of mine. He is five feet, two inches in height and pug nosed. Two enormous wild bear tusks stand out like hat pegs from his punctured ear lobes. His heavy earrings are of brass. Since childhood, they have stretched the lower part of his lobes, until now they are two inches longer than mine. His only covering, apart from a loincloth, is a festoon of beads around his neck and black grass bands around his legs just below the knees. He is just literate, which is a notable achievement, for literacy comes with the gospel."

It's easy to think of this man as a quaint hangover from the past, a "wild man" from Borneo. Yet he is a proclaimer, one able to use the Scriptures, his only book. He's a man who is obedient to every scrap of light that the Scriptures bring him. To such, God keeps his promise and gives further understanding (John 7:17).

Our culture demands serious training in order to be a "professional" leader. Once we have the training, we feel that we are not honoring God or our people unless we exercise our gifts to bless the body. Where fishermen were preachers, teachers, and apostles in the first century, now we must have degreed professionals.

There are two problems here. First, no man has a spiritual ministry by virtue of his education. Worse, the willingness of the layperson to teach decreases the more the professionals exercise their gifts. What lab technician or accountant wants to be compared to the professional speaker? The equipping environment, where the message of a fisherman could carry as much weight as the Bible college graduate, has been destroyed.

It's the task of leaders to release and empower the word to every member of the body. Think what an impact we'll make on the world when we allow George, the printer, the freedom to stand in the pulpit and share his story. It will impact the world.

Professionalism also means that we insist on looking and sounding respectable. We want the sermon neatly laid out with logical flow and three main points. If we insist on this being the highest goal, we will achieve it. We may have wonderful sounding sermons, but will they touch the heart? What will we lose in the process?

Today we suffer from the cultural impact of individualism. We have lost the biblical perspective on the life of the Spirit in the community. Living in our western atomistic and cause/effect world, we have limited the life of the Spirit too much to the individual. Paul would have placed far more emphasis on the Spirit in the body (cf. I Corinthians10:17, 11:29). We need to discern the body. Jesus is no longer an individual; He is the gathered power of the community. We need a new understanding of the corporate presence of Christ. *"Where two or three are gathered in My name, there am I among them."*

Conclusion

Change is often messy, and few of us like change. It's a challenge to all of us to release control and allow new ways of doing and being to arise. Leaders are needed to correct, protect, and direct as the body of Christ is equipped and released. In the first two centuries, the church grew and spread like wild fire (apart from buildings and programs) because *all* God's people carried the good news. The modern house-church movement is attempting to recover the dynamic of that day.

New wine requires new wineskins; otherwise, the skins will burst and the wine will be lost. The Lord Himself is bringing change to structures. His heart is to see all His people released to serve Him. Old structures are falling down, and God is raising up a new generation of leaders who are not afraid to try new ways and to walk without maps, depending on the Him.

Nehemiah was the prototype builder. He walked with integrity, courage, and wisdom, with dependence on the Lord. He walked as an equal among brothers; although, he had the right to ask for honor and privilege. He was instrumental in rebuilding the temple as a place where God could dwell.

We need to prepare our hearts to be ready for the coming Reformation: the liberation of body life in the power of the Spirit!

"The God of heaven Himself will prosper us; therefore we His servants will arise and build...." (Ezra 2:20).

Chapter 29
Building Community

There's a story told about the Apostle John who spoke often to his disciples about love. One day, in exasperation, someone said, "John, why do you always talk about love?" Smiling, John responded, "Because, it's the most needful thing!" (1 John 3:16-19)

Love is the common ingredient in most of our searching and longing. We seek wholeness, to know and become all that we can be. All of us, in one way or another, seek significant, real community, a place to belong and a place to call "home." We sense at a deep level that our own healing is bound up with the healing of others; we know that the journey toward wholeness is personal but also communal. We know that Jesus does not have just a body; He *is* the body, and we are His members.

Ministry is the Creation of Space for Community to Develop

My wife and I have been involved in many small groups over the past few years. We have sought to create safety for people, and we have wrestled with traditional concepts of authority and leadership, looking for a balance between form and freedom while seeking to include the traditional elements of church life in our groups.

In the process, we've heard some encouraging testimonies. First, a single mother who had drifted around the edges of the church told us one day, "I feel like I've come home." Then a young couple that had never been committed to a small group before told us, "We feel like we've found a place to belong." A few weeks later as we finished praying for another mom, she told us that for the first time she had been able to share her fears. We were deeply touched. We knew that the strength of the group did not depend on us, but the life of Christ was being seen and felt among us as we made space for Him.

But wait a second, you thought I was talking about the creation of space for community, and now I am talking about space for Jesus. In reality, these two are one because Jesus indwells His body.

The Gathered Power of God

Consider these words from Karl Rahner, a Catholic theologian: "Church is the place where the gathered weakness of man becomes the gathered power of God." Or consider these words from Jim Wallis, of the Sojourner's community: "The chief lesson of community is that God breaks through at the weak places." Sound familiar? How about this one: *"Most gladly then I will boast in my weakness, for when I am weak, then He is strong"* (2 Corinthians 12:10).

It's amazing how rarely I connect deeply with others around my strengths! When I really do a great job of teaching or writing, I find myself admired, but rarely loved. When I am sharing my struggles, doubts or fears with a friend or two, I find myself supported, loved, and encouraged. I find myself connected, loving and supporting in turn. Isn't it odd?

In 1 Corinthians 12, Paul says, *"the weak parts are more needful."* A few years ago at the Seattle Special Olympics, nine contestants, all physically or mentally disabled, assembled at the starting line for the 100-yard dash. At the gun they all started out, not exactly in a dash, but with a relish to run the race to the finish and win. All, that is, except one little boy who stumbled on the asphalt, tumbled over a couple of times, and began to cry. The other eight heard the boy cry. They slowed down and looked back. Then they all turned around and went back, every one of them.

One girl with Down's Syndrome bent down and kissed him and said, "This will make it better." Then all nine linked arms and walked together to the finish line. Everyone in the stadium stood, and the cheering went on for several minutes. People who were there are still telling the story. Why? Because deep down we know this one thing: What matters in this life is more than winning for ourselves. What matters in this life is helping others win, even if it means slowing down to help them up.

I believe that much of the work the Lord wants to do in the lives of leaders is to teach them to walk in their weakness as powerfully as they walk in their strengths. It's easy (and tempting) to share victories as a way to call others to discipleship. It's difficult (and humbling) to share our weaknesses as a way of glorifying God, but He puts His glory in pots of clay for just that purpose!

Let's face it, sharing our struggles feels like weakness! Vulnerability doesn't come naturally for most of us, and it feels, well, vulnerable!

If my weaknesses glorify Christ, then the concept of leadership is on an entirely different footing. Maybe it's okay to have a non-professional in the pulpit. Maybe the sermon doesn't have to have three perfectly flowing points. Maybe the weaker parts are more needful even in ministry. Maybe we really are a body, and the ministry of each individual really is important (radical thought!). We need to recover Eph.4:16, where the body is built "as each part does its work." As Markus Barth put it, "It is at the point of connection that Jesus is made known."[xviii]

I can't count the number of gifted preachers I have heard who touched my intellect, then someone shared a testimony that related in some way to the teaching, and I found my heart in my mouth. When Buddy Bell, a minister from the Landmark church in Montgomery, Alabama, spoke on his congregation's growth through small groups, he used a powerful illustration when he gave two couples from his congregation the floor.[xix] They believed in the method simply because they were brought to Christ through the meshing of their lives with others in their group. They, not Buddy, made the most effective points. Buddy Bell couldn't compete with the new converts as they told their stories and cried about a ministry that saved them and their marriages. If we believe that the word of God must come only through leaders, we have not yet understood the corporate reality of Christ, nor have we really heard Peter's first sermon at Pentecost. The "point of connection" is usually a place of openness, a place of weakness where we have a need.

Valuing Every Member

Part of creating safety is creating space where each member is valued and validated as having a unique contribution. Be careful that the most gifted don't dominate because you will lose something you cannot easily recover.

I participate regularly in a small group where the leader leads in a coaching style, and is often invisible unless correction is needed. Like coaches, we often sit on the sidelines and merely observe the game. Like lifeguards at the pool, we are ready to jump into the water when necessary! Isaac Stern uses an analogy from his life as a conductor that beautifully pictures the role of leadership in our gatherings:

The conductor is not a powerful person. It appears so, but it is not so. On the surface it seems that the music is produced by the power of the conductor to tell everyone what to do and when to do it. He may have to do that, but it is not what makes the music. (If he does too much directing, the real music will not be heard, but only his own idea of it.)

A good conductor does not merely tell everyone what to do; rather he helps everyone to hear what is so. For this he is not primarily a telling but a listening individual: even while the orchestra is performing loudly, he is listening inwardly to silent music. He is not so much commanding as he is obedient.

The conductor conducts by being conducted. He first hears, feels, loses himself in the silent music; then when he knows what it is, he finds a way to help others hear it, too. He knows that music is not made by people playing instruments, but rather by music playing people.

At some of our meetings there is a wonderful harmony, but occasionally the tuba risks drowning out the softer tones of the flute. At our last meeting, one of the tubas was dominant in the wrong place, blaring out a note that was discordant and disturbing. When that happens, we need to take the tuba aside and show it "a more excellent way." If you have a group where someone is a tuba, no matter how beautifully he plays, you may have to limit his participation so that you can also hear the softer tones of the flute. Power is perfected in weakness, and the weak are easily intimidated by dominant leaders with more verbal gifts.

At the level of weakness, we are truly one. In our strengths we stand alone, independent not only from God, but from one another. Where I am strong, I don't need my brother or my sister. Unneeded, they are unconnected. Where I am weak, I need them. Then together we are strong. Our weaknesses hold the power of connection and the glory of God. Our strengths hold only our own potential.

Form and Freedom

One simple question relates to form and freedom. Do our structures facilitate the purpose of our meeting: to build community and release the ministry of Jesus? We must remain flexible if we are going to allow the Lord to do His work. Jean Vanier comments, "So we have to create structures which encourage everyone to participate, and especially the shy people. Those who have the most light to shed often dare not show it; they are afraid of appearing stupid. They do not recognize their own gift, perhaps because others haven't recognized it either."xx

With too much structure, people will feel stifled, and God will have a hard time breaking into your meeting. With too little structure, people may feel uncomfortable and wonder if anyone is in control. Too much freedom is like driving without a map—people never know where they are; too much oversight is like walking on eggshells—people won't feel safe taking risks and will let the leader do it all. Letty Russell shares:

"Recently I taught in a continuing education program for church professionals on the west coast. In one of the sessions we tried out a model of contextual Bible study that was based on a mutual sharing of life stories and situations that seemed to illuminate the text and its context. One minister raised his hand and said, 'I try to get others to speak in Bible study, but the women, and sometimes even the men, defer to me as having authority. What should I do?'"

The solution proposed demystifies structures. Every important issue in our lives is embedded in social, economic, political, and religious structures. To work toward partnership in community, we must analyze the way these forces shape our understanding of reality and our use of authority. The minister mentioned needed to understand the structures of church and community life that lead to a hierarchical understanding of teaching and decision-making. If he had understood, he would not have expected women to speak out simply because he requested it.

In order to work as partners, people need to be political. That is, they need to look at the way power and authority are functioning in their group and in the larger institutions in order to be able to understand how decision-making works and who should be held accountable. Without such knowledge of structures, people will continue to be dependent on those who rule "for them."

Gnosticism and Spirituality

Don't be too spiritual! Gnosticism is an old heresy, and Gnostics claimed special knowledge about God. In the first century this group claimed that Christ didn't really take on flesh because they believed that matter was evil. So God didn't really suffer and die on the cross, He only appeared to suffer and die.

Sometimes I feel Christians become hyper-spiritual, denying the importance of matter. This is not pleasing to God, and it is dangerous to those around us! God really did take flesh, and Jesus was fully human. He died to redeem our whole body, soul, and spirit. To emphasize a literal incarnation, John writes,

> *That which was from the beginning,*
> *Which we have heard,*
> *Which we have seen with our eyes,*
> *Which we have looked upon,*
> *And our hands have handled,*
> *Concerning the word of life –*
> *The life was manifested, and we have seen*
> *and bear witness,*
> *And declare to you that eternal life which was with the*
> *Father and was manifested to us.*
> (1 John 1: 1-2)

God invented matter. It was His idea! We live in a real world and sometimes the most spiritual thing to do is a very human thing—to rest, to cry, to laugh, to sit by a waterfall, to give someone flowers, or to share a coffee. Love is a human and practical matter because we are physical beings.

Living in a material world also means that symbols are important. The Lord gave us bread and wine to remember Him to teach us that ordinary things become Holy. Material things are also an aid to faith. The arts are important for the sake of celebration but also because they bring matter and spirit together. The arts are a metaphor of incarnation.

Hold the Word and the Spirit together. It's because we are a unity of body, soul, and spirit that a course on communication can not only change a marriage but revolutionize our life with God! Take time to be normal; build relationships founded on mutual respect and honesty.

From Community to the Nations

Jim Wallis wrote, "The ability of people to move to a new place tomorrow depends on the love and acceptance they feel today. Community is the place where the healing of our own lives becomes the foundation for the healing of the nations."[xxi]

Mission only has integrity when our own houses are in order. What use is it to preach a message we haven't lived ourselves? St. Francis said that we should "preach the gospel at all times, if necessary, use words!"

There is a natural cycle in community that mirrors the cleansing cycle within the human body. The blood flows inward to the liver for cleansing and then to the heart to receive oxygen. Next the heart pumps that life-giving blood outward to every member of the body. Finally, when it has done its work, it flows inward for cleansing again.

In the same way there is a natural dynamic of inward and outward life in the body of Christ. There is no foundation for outreach without community, and there is no healthy community apart from growth. Jim Wallis writes, "Both vision and nurture are keys to community. Without nurture, a community will soon exhaust itself in pursuit of the vision. Without vision, a community will become stuck in self-preoccupation and travel in circles. With only vision a community soon loses any real quality of love. With only nurture the community forgets what its love is for."

Let's give John the final word: *"Beloved, let us love one another, For love is of God, and everyone who loves is born of God and knows God"* (1 John 4:7).

Chapter 30
God So Loved The World; Why Can't The Church?

One of the greatest cultural shifts in the history of humanity is taking place in our lifetime, and if the church is going to claim this new world for Christ, it must adjust.

For the past five hundred years, the church has taught the gospel in the culture of modernism, where the worldview was rational, logical, linear, and book-based, but that world is collapsing and a whole new world is being born.

The postmodern generation has a greater interest in spiritual things than the modernist. They're ravenous for real experiences and emotional fulfillment. Yet the paradox is that this culture has a lack of interest in church things. Our inability to communicate the gospel in interesting ways has caused this culture to turn it's back on Christianity. Gospel content should always remain the same, but it's paramount that we adjust our style of communication. For too long the church has acted as if culture should come to our buildings and learn our peculiar language, our way of doing things, and then we'll let them become disciples of Jesus.

Postmodern people experience God in different ways from "modern" people. In the modern world everything in worship is reduced mainly to the visual sense, but post-moderns need more than the visual. They need to hear God, smell God, taste God, and touch God. The Pentecostals and the Eastern Orthodox are doing this best, with Pentecostals using their bodies in worship and Eastern Orthodox having "the smells and the bells." Communication in a post-modern culture needs to be experiential, participatory, image-based, and connective. This "karaoke culture" isn't looking for rationalism. It wants participation, not the performance-based "sit-and-soak" worship of the modern era. It's a generation that thinks in images, not in words.

Because people are being connected with one another globally through the Internet, it will be the key source for relationships in the twenty-first century. The church, therefore, must move from modernism's "highly individualistic" expressions of worship and learn to approach in ways that connect people to each other and to God in richer and deeper ways. That is done through music, the arts, and technology.

Just as the modern church system for learning and faith has been based on books, the new church will be image-based as well as connected to the digital realities of the postmodern culture. God will create a new church, if needed, to be in this future. Whether it will be the church as we know it — that's another matter.

Chapter 31
An Uncommon Vision

The makers of the *Palm Pilot* obviously saw something coming, something others didn't see. Power in the palm. Interesting. We're only now seeing the beginning of a new revolution in the customized calendar. If you control your calendar, you control your life. Your calendar can make or break you. The pilots at *Palm* saw this.

The church has to ask, "What is on our calendar?" If our church has a "pilot," how far does it see? What does it see? What kind of vision do we have for contributing to our community? Church leaders must ask some hard questions.

The fact is that if we don't have something truly unique to offer, we should just close up shop. It will require an uncommon vision to reach the unchurched and to restore the overchurched. It's that simple. They know as well as you that Jesus and the world has had enough of tradition. What the church of the twenty-first century needs is a "lotta" love!

The Status Quo church is pretty much museum material to this culture that likes to see, feel, touch, taste, and hear life. They are looking for experience, and the funny thing is, the church has basically denied that Jesus can be experienced. Only recently has that changed. No, we've not found the "miracle cure," but we have started helping people "experience" Jesus.

The Bible makes a statement that has been selected and used effectively by a new generation of evangelists, "Without vision, people will perish." More appropriate for us, without *uncommon* vision, the Christian community will perish.

Reaching the unchurched and restoring the overchurched may not seem that radical in concept, but it is in contrast to the way church has traditionally been done. Most Church of Christ people have "experienced" church but have not "experienced" Jesus. They have merely been shouted at with the message of Jesus.

The vision of a new generation is to love like Jesus loved, churched or unchurched.

Chapter 32
Engaging the World Through The Senses

I recently read a book by Tex Sample entitled, *The Spectacle of Worship in a Wired World*. His basic thesis is that the electronic culture has changed the way in which Boomers, Xers, and Millennials engage with their world and that our worship will need to adapt.

Understanding why each generation approaches worship in its own unique way is critical if the emerging Churches of Christ are going to teach Jesus in contemporary culture.

Engaging the World Through Image

Earlier generations grew up in an oral world where they engaged the world through proverbs, stories, and relationships. Issues were dealt with in terms of their effect on their family, neighbors, and the relationships, they had. After this there came a literate world where people thought in terms of propositional claims, theory, and conceptualization, and where they developed ideas in linear discourse. But the Boomers, Xers, and Millennials grew up in a post-literate, electronic world. They think in terms of images, sound, and visualization. It is significant to note that those who have been most influenced by electronic culture participate in church at far lower levels than those of previous generations.

Our senses are historically and socially organized. They are conditioned and influenced by the period of time in which we live and by the culture of which we are a part. For example, the Greeks specialized in sight, the Hebrews in hearing, the modern west in visual, the Koreans in taste, and today's electronic culture in sound. People today are wired differently. Media has shaped the western world through television and the Internet. There are three components in an electronic culture:

- Images
- Sound
- Visualization

In one sense, thinking in images is not new. Newspapers and art have been around a long time, but people don't "read" images as they once did. No longer does the contemporary western world listen to discursive messages. The shift from the printed word to image has had an impact on how people think about salvation. Communicating the gospel in a constant flow of images that are ever changing will soon replace the coherent, orderly arrangement of ideas. The subjective must come before the objective; if it doesn't, we will lose our audience.

Engaging the World Through Sound

The West continues to engage its world through the visual, as reflected in the phrases, "I see what you mean!" or "Listen to my point of view!" But new metaphors, such as "I hear you saying!" or "I hear you!" are being used more and more, which suggests that emphasis is not only visual but also musical.

Popular culture, with its music, has brought a growing emphasis on sound. Rhythm has become a vital part of the new generation. Music use to have an emphasis on the first and third beats of a four/four rock and roll song (e.g., BOOM dah, BOOM dah). In the mid 1960s this changed to a focus on the upbeat (e.g., un CHAW, un CHAW). The way people clap differently either on the upbeat or downbeat shows their different generations. We are wired differently. What speaks to my grandpa does not speak to me. What moves me, entertains me, and touches me, doesn't do the same for them. And we won't engage the younger generation until we concede that along with images, sound as beat is critical to them.

Engaging the World Though Visualization

Technological developments, consumer trends, and the increasing role of films and video are aspects of a significant move toward visualization in everyday life. The electronic culture and screen introduced an entire range of practices not previously present to the world. MTV, film, and TV are more visual than audio. Teenagers are even called "screenagers" today. While print-viewing habits have changed (fewer youths read books or newspapers), other more visual activities have increased among them (visits to museums or galleries). This affects the way people make judgments about truth and reality. They look and learn through visual influences rather than rational arguments or mathematical proofs.

These three ways of engaging the world are combined to create a new powerful way of communicating. *Spectacle Creations* aren't just presentations by performers but events that provide an occasion for the enactment of an experience by participants and large crowds that gather. In this spectacle there is the development of anticipation or expectation about what is coming; there is pacing (a movement from fast to slow to fast); there is total participation by the audience. Music plays a key part of the spectacle. Sound, as a sensual component, enters us in a way in which the visual alone cannot. Previous generations found meaning in words; today's generations find meaning in experiences.

In concerts there is a convergence—the total experience takes place in the response of an audience to the multidimensional character of electronic events. There are music, words, the charisma of the artists, the percussive use of light, images and beat, the behaviors of the crowd, the kinesthetic involvement of the audience in moving, dancing and typically staying on their feet the entire time. The power of the event for the participative audience occurs in the convergence of the sensory experience. They are drawn into a vortex of personal and social yearnings and satisfactions.

When you get people in close proximity to one another, focus their attention on a common object, and engage them in exercises that arouse emotions, bonding occurs. This is the power of spectacle. Spectacle is the ultimate experience where convergence generates participation and meaning. The following features of Spectacle are noted:

- Spectacle creates convergence, which is cognitive and dynamic, while knowing is generated through light and visualization. This knowing is a source of identity.
- Spectacle develops emotional bonds and a sense of being part of something much bigger than you.
- Spectacle reflects and enacts the lives of those gathered—it is a dramatization.
- Spectacle generates commitment and convictions—these can be good or bad.
- Spectacles create bonding—with whom you gather determines with whom you will be bonded.

But spectacle tends to create publics, not communities, since a common story is not provided. People bring their own stories with them to the event.

Ministering Incarnationally

The church has to "pitch tent" (incarnate) with the electronic culture, yet it must be transformative, not conformative. It must bring its own story, tradition, and practices into the equation. The church lives in a culture and is a culture. This presents the church with the difficult task of incarnating with a culture while remaining true to its story. God became flesh and joined the indigenous practices of the culture of Jesus' time. The word became flesh and "pitched a tent." Flesh is encoded culturally and historically and is socially constructed. Depending on the time and place in which we live, our senses are organized differently. Approaches to feelings and forms of reason change with time.

In pitching the tent, Jesus experienced an indigenous engagement. But at the same time, Jesus didn't pitch a tent with every practice, and the church cannot pitch a tent with every practice it finds in a culture. However, it must not be so captive to a range of cultural practices, which are acceptable yet outdated, that it imposes them on another culture in colonial fashion. Often the church identifies practices as essential to the faith when they are basically an expression of pitching tent in another, quite different culture.

The implications of this are profound and far-reaching. First, the incarnation is not God joining the human story and becoming part of it, but it's the disclosure that the world is part of God's story. We must understand our picture in terms of God's greater picture. Secondly, God's story is fleshy and engaged with human practices, which means the emerging Church of Christ must take seriously the fleshy use of images, sound, and visualization. It must pitch a tent through the practices of convergence, bonding, and commitment.

Chapter 33
A First Century Postmodernist

They brought Jesus to Pilate insisting He was worthy of death. The Jews needed Pilate's approval, but Pilate seems confused by their request. What has this man done? Is he a king? Jesus' answer confuses Pilate even more:

"My kingdom is not of this world. If it were, my servants would fight to prevent my arrest by the Jews. But now my kingdom is from another place" (John 18:36).

Pilate is even more confused.

"You are a king, then!" said Pilate. Jesus answered, *"You are right in saying I am a king. In fact, for this reason I was born, and for this I came into the world, to testify to the truth. Everyone on the side of truth listens to me."*

Pilate responds as a true Postmodernist, *"What is truth?" (John 18:38).* The echoes of that question are found in the writings of Nietzsche, Lyotard, Foucault, Derrida, and indeed in contemporary culture. Bill Clinton might add, "Well, that depends on your definition of *is*.

Is Christianity Modern or Postmodern?

Sometimes you get the impression that Christians would like to claim either the modern era or the postmodern era for themselves. Conservative evangelical forces are displaying a sentiment that says, in a loud and clear voice, that things were better at some point in time in the past. If only we could go back to the more blissful times of the 1950s and the 1960s when everyone believed in God and the terrible vices of homosexuality and abortion didn't exist, we would be happy. If it's true, and it is, that we are observing the emergence of the postmodern era, these "time-tunnel Christians" would like very much for it to go away. Even if they could remember that the modern era wasn't exactly a hospitable context for those who believed in the existence and acts of a supernatural God, they view the postmodern era as infinitely worse. They ask, "Can't we stay in the modern era?" They reject postmodernism believing it is anti-Christian while falsely accepting modernism as better.

On the other side, we encounter Christians who can scarcely resist doing a little dance at the demise of modernism. Thank goodness, that terrible era is over! They remember how opposed the modern era was to Christians and how rationalism and individualism reigned supreme. They see the postmodern era as one of boundless opportunities. The emphasis on story, the understanding that in the end everything comes down to faith as opposed to certainty, and the renewed pursuit of community all point to a more receptive ideology for the Christian community to speak the message of the cross.

Maybe I'm overstating my case, but I believe two distinct groups of Christians can be observed today. While no one has been burned at the stake yet, one side often has that "you-people-have-left-the-truth" feeling, while the other side sneeringly dismisses the faithless Christianity of the modern era."

The postmodern Christians are very uncomfortable with Jerry Falwell's denouncement of the Teletubbies, while the modern era Christians applaud James Dobson's weekly solicitations for Christians to take a more aggressive stance on the issues of school prayer, pro-life, and the protection of our society from the gay agenda. As it becomes more and more obvious that our world is indeed entering the postmodern era, a polarization is taking place within Christianity between those who fear what they see as the coming darkness and those who rejoice in what they hold to be the dawn of a new era.

A Kingdom That Transcends Earthly Kingdoms, Empires, and Eras

Jesus' kingdom is not of this world. Pilate doesn't get it and neither do many modern and postmodern people. Eager either to claim Jesus for themselves or quickly to dispose of him, they meet in Jesus a King who announces a Kingdom that is from beyond this world. Jesus offends the Pharisees and their strict sense of correct theology, and he just confuses Pilate, whose view of truth is relative at best.

In Pilate's defense, he does try (with true postmodern passion) to get the innocent set free. It is obvious that Jesus poses no threat to the Roman Empire, and that is all Pilate is worried about. I imagine that Pilate may have wondered if Jesus was a nutcase, but he makes an effort to have Jesus released by juxtaposing him with Barabbas who is a known murderer.

The Jewish leaders shake their fists, rally the crowd, and shout their demands, causing Pilate to wash his hands in water (sort of the ultimate postmodern denial of reality: if I wash my hands in water, it's like it never happened). And Jesus is on his way to the cross, where by dying, he inaugurates a Kingdom that at the climax of time will consume all Kingdoms and eras.

Since the death and resurrection of Jesus, almost two thousand years of world history have passed and with them many kingdoms and empires. The church has faired better in some areas than in others, being ever forced to adapt to a changing world that it cannot call home, but unable for the moment to go to the place that it does call home.

The irony of the situation isn't easy. We wonder where we belong and how we as Christians can live *in* the world without being *of* it. That question is being asked more frequently now that we are going through such dramatic changes. Living where two tectonic plates meet always creates a sense of insecurity; when those plates move and the ground quakes beneath our feet, it is difficult to stand still and just hold on to the things we've always known. Earthquakes have a destructive effect on the things we've traditionally trusted.

Three World Views

So who are we? Where do we belong? Are we modernists, holding to a sense of fundamentalism? Are we postmoderns, who see everything as mere perspective? Or are we neither, just simply Christians committed to Jesus and His way?

I believe Christianity, modernism, and postmodernism could best be illustrated as three intersecting circles. Each of these circles intersects partly with one other circle. Let me give you a few examples. Particular to Christianity are the kingdom of God, faith in heaven and hell, and the idea of the existence of God. These are concepts that Christianity shares with neither modernism nor postmodernism, but Christianity intersects with modernism in a number of areas. Both believe in the power and necessity of reason, the value of empirical research, and the existence of an objective world, to name a few. Likewise, Christianity intersects with postmodernism, albeit in different areas. The value narrative, the spiritual world, the need for experience, and the power of faith are common principles that intersect. Modernism and postmodernism intersect also. They both reject the biblical world view, the pursuit of human happiness as the chief of all pursuits, a trust in the human power to bring about a better society, the scientific pursuit, and the search for a political strategy to organize society in a way that benefits all.

There seems to be a *holistic* (and dare I say more *objective*) view of this current moment in human history, a perspective that seems to be a kinder point of view. I speak of kindness here because the nature of world views and cultures is such that we often tend to speak of traditions other than our own in a condescending and scornful manner. We have simply had a difficult time in disagreeing with other folks without displaying a strong dose of derailment and cynicism. Our own beliefs and positions have made it difficult to believe that others could be motivated by the desire to do good, when they arrive at such different conclusions than we.

When we come to understand that our world view predisposes us to a critical and unfair view of others, it becomes a biblical mandate to move beyond rigid positions to a more tolerant position. I pray that as we grow in our understanding, we will move away from our "world-view-bound criticism."

A Lesson the Impeachment Trial Can Teach Us

A clear example of "world-view-bound criticism" became obvious during the impeachment trial of President Clinton. There was no way the Republicans were going to believe that the Democrats were motivated by the desire to do what was best for the country. In their minds, they were convinced that all the Democrats wanted to do was to protect their President. Conversely, the Democrats could not understand why the Republicans wanted to oust the President purely because of moral reasons as opposed to partisan reasons. The situation became increasingly polarized, and it became harder and harder to see that on both sides of the issue there were, in fact, those whose chief concern was for the country, not their party.

Seeing Each Other

A similar situation has occurred in the Churches of Christ who sit on the edge of the twenty-first century. The words "conservative" and "liberal" are once again being used in disparaging ways. Perhaps they always were, but it seems the tension is renewing itself, and the lines of demarcation seem clearer and clearer. It's important that we remember that the Kingdom of God is not of this world. It is neither modern nor postmodern, though it intersects both. Modernism is already passing, and postmodernism will eventually pass, but the Kingdom of God is eternal. Everyone who is on the side of truth listens to Jesus (John 18:37), no matter his time in history.

Chapter 34
Present/Future Leaders

The valor of leadership involves having the courage to face reality, then helping the people around you face reality. It's no accident that the word "vision" refers to one's capacity to see. Of course, in the church, vision has come to mean something more abstract and appealing, but the quality of any vision depends on its accuracy, not just on its appeal or on how imaginative it is.

Mustering the courage to interrogate reality is a leader's central function, which requires the courage to face three realities at once:

- First, to ask what values do we stand for and are there gaps between those values and how we actually behave?
- Second, to ask what are the strengths and talents of our congregation, and are there gaps between our resources and what our surrounding culture demands?
- Third, to ask what opportunities does the future hold, and are there gaps between those opportunities and our ability to capitalize on them?

Present/future leaders don't answer these questions themselves. That was the old style of leadership which had all the answers encased in its own personal vision, with everything else being a sales job to persuade the people to sign up for it. Leaders certainly provide direction (often meaning they pose well-structured questions rather than offering definitive answers). Imagine the differences in behavior between leaders who operate with the idea that "leadership means influencing the congregation to follow the leader's vision" and those who operate with the idea that "leadership means influencing the congregation to face its problems and to live into its opportunities." Mobilizing the followship to tackle tough challenges is what defines and shapes the role of the new spiritual leader.

Navigating the Reality of Conflict and Mobilizing Congregations

Church leaders tend to be allergic to conflict, particularly in the older established congregations where members have know each other for eons. Being averse to conflict is understandable. Conflict is dangerous. It can damage relationships; it can threaten congregational stability. But conflict is the primary engine of creativity and innovation. People don't learn by staring into a mirror; people learn by encountering difference. So hand in hand with the courage to face reality comes the courage to orchestrate conflicts when they arise.

Leaders of the present/future need to "have the stomach" for conflict and uncertainty, among their people and within themselves. That is why present/future leaders need to have an experimental mind-set. Some decisions will work, some won't. Some ministries will move forward, some won't. But every decision and every mission will teach you and your church something about how the world is changing.

In other words, facing reality means facing up to mistakes and failures – especially your own failures. In the mid-1990s, Bill Gates made a big decision about the Internet. He decided that the Net wasn't going to be all that important. Then he changed his decision because the people to whom he was listening contradicted his earlier decision. In the mid-1980s, Ken Olsen, the co-founder of Digital Equipment Corporation, decided that personal computers weren't going to be all that important. He didn't change his decision very quickly, and Digital suffered as a result. These days, leaving any big decision in one person's hands is like playing Russian roulette. It's much safer to run multiple experiments. You never know which ideas are going to flourish and which ones are going to die.

If the role of the leader is first to help people face reality and then to mobilize them to make change, then one of the questions that defines both of those tasks is this: What's precious, and what's expendable?[xxii] Is a lectern in front of an audience an absolute or is it expendable? Is the traditional invitation song so precious to our heritage that we dare not tinker? Are the old modern-era Church of Christ traditions expendable, or are those traditions so precious and central to our core identity that irreversible loss will be the result of any change? Should future/present leadership accommodate "neo-traditional?"[xxiii] At the highest level, the mission of a leader should be to inform and assist the body of Christ in discerning tradition, culture, and scripture, determining what's changeable and what's unchangeable.

The civil-rights movement posed several questions: What's most precious about America? What values do we stand for? Do we stand for freedom and equal opportunity or do we stand for how we are living today? By posing those questions in such terms, Martin Luther King, Jr. and the movement's other strategists generated conflict within the hearts and minds of many people around the country. People faced an internal contradiction between the values they espoused and the way they lived. Millions of people had to decide for themselves what was precious about their country and what was expendable about the supremacist lessons that they had learned.

Chapter 35
New Maps for a New World

You and I happen to be living on the "edge" of a time of high "tectonic activity" in history, the end of one age and the beginning of another. It's a time of shaking. Yesterday's maps are already outdated, and today's soon will be. The uncharted world ahead of us is what we will call "the new world on the other side": the other side of two world wars and one cold war, the other side of communism, the other side of the second millennium, and the other side of modernism. There used to be an Old World, then a New World, then the Third World, but now all three are being swept up in a new world.

During the last hundred years, and especially the last fifty, old-world technology has intensified cultural pressures and unleashed tremor after tremor, each far more significant than could ever have been imagined. These technological tremors have helped bring to an end the old world that created them. Think of the automobile and its effects on the environment, the economy, the family unit, and even courtship and sexuality (especially when the car is equipped with a back seat). Think of radio, air travel, birth-control pills, antibiotics, and the cathode ray tube; we're barely past the mid-century mark. Then came the tidal wave of social change set in motion during the sixties. No wonder the old maps don't fit the new world!

New Theology

We live in a time when the old systematic theologies are fading. They are not surviving the transition well. Actually, a new theology has been, in some seminal form, alive and well among us already for quite some time. In the middle of the twentieth century, C.S. Lewis expressed early articulations of it in essays and, even better, in fiction. Now, at the end of the second millennium, one feels the new theology moving in the Churches of Christ.

This new era demands that our theology be resurrected to a new life, and not just as a technical matter, but as a creative pursuit with passionate inquiry, like the best art and the best science. Psychology, sociology, the new physics, history, comparative religion, and spirituality, not to mention postmodernism in general, all are calling for some creative Christian leaders to unfold some new paradigms for us to use in our explorations. The old systems feel tired, used up, and worn out, but the thirst for God is as strong as ever. Am I calling for new wineskins? Yes, but new wine will be required if we're going to navigate the dynamics of a new time.

Whenever a new theology begins replacing a past theology, we see some "things" emerge along side the changes, things like creative thinking, a new and energetic pursuit of truth, and a fresh and revitalized exploring that replaces the old memorized, repeated, and often defended legalistic doctrines we have relied upon for years. What a challenge we encounter when we open ourselves up to discover how Jesus Christ wants to theologically incarnate himself for the postmodern world, just as he did for the post-Enlightenment world of the old church.

What Must We Do?

Postmodernism is the intellectual boundary between the old world and the other side. Why is it so important? Because when your view of truth is changed, when your confidence in the human ability to know truth in any objective way is revolutionized, then everything changes, including theology (and not only the content and categories of your theology). More far-reaching, the mind of the person doing and learning theology is also changed. We have the same basic data, but different software and different hardware changes everything.

I recently read an interview with a popular Christian apologist. When he was asked what he thought of postmodernism, he answered, "It must be opposed at all costs." Then came the follow-up question: Why? "Because it destroys our apologetic."

I thought, "Thank God this guy is over sixty; he can afford to think that postmodernism can be opposed." But those in touch with their culture realize that opposing postmodernism is as futile as opposing the English language. It's here. It's reality. It's the future. It's not only a fact on the event horizon; it's the way this generation processes every other fact on the event horizon. What are we going to do about it, with it, in it?

So one of the biggest questions on my screen these days is, "How does the Spirit of Jesus Christ incarnate in a postmodern world?" This question very likely terrifies or infuriates some Christians because they see the traumatic implications of what I am saying. And maybe they are right. Maybe there is no way ahead. Maybe the faithful thing to do these days is to become intellectually Amish and create communities that live in the past.

However, in spite of my fear, I have this faith that if we push forward through this transition time, some of us may find a good land for the Christian faith on the other side. Yes, it will require courage, creativity, honesty, and humility as well as Christian leaders becoming more like the best artists and scientists, passionately devoted to truth, but less politically inclined to continue doing things the "way we have always done them" because of the church across town.

Chapter 36
Let's Call Her What We Want Her to Be, a Minister

Shelley Neilson

I am at home in the Church of Christ. While I have heard and seen facets of our religious tradition that have caused me to cringe; there are other features that have persuaded me to cling to my religious roots. I like the fact that we are believers committed to understanding the cross and what it means to the world and that we remember that transforming event on a weekly basis. It is important to me that we continually explore scripture, allowing the inspired word of God to be new every morning. I am strengthened to be part of the body of Christ, many members gifted and called to service according to the Spirit to fulfill the purposes of God. I like the fact that as autonomous congregations we have the freedom to continually reexamine our lives together in light of scripture and with respect to the tradition of those who have gone before. These characteristics describe a heritage of which I am proud to belong.

As I look back on the journey that has brought me to here and now. I am still caught by surprise. I would not have imagined in my childhood or youth, as I entertained visions of a career as a writer or actress or lawyer, that I would find myself employed as a minister by any church, certainly not a church of Christ. However, God has ways that we cannot fathom. As I reflect on the people and episodes that shaped me over the years, I cannot deny the sense that I was prepared to be here in this place (Portland, Oregon) at this particular time in the history of our tradition. A time of transition, of reevaluation, some call it renewal; a time when we seem to be revisiting what it means to be Christians only and not the only Christians.

I am a member of a congregation that is "in many ways a pioneering church because we are taking the less traveled road. We look for renewing norms within our own story/tradition, in our case 'a people of the book.' Allowing a fresh, disciplined appropriation of scripture to provide models for renewal."[xxiv] In the face of a culture swiftly separating itself from values that not many years ago were shared by church and society, this community (East County Church of Christ) has not dug its heels in and insisted that we do things the way they have always been done. Nor have we rushed to adopt a packaged improvement plan, to apply a church growth model that has succeeded elsewhere and is sure to "double our attendance in no time." Instead, our sincere desire has been to discern, as a body, the kind of congregation God has called us to be.

By looking at who we are (corporately and individually), by examining the gifts members have and desire to use in service to the church, by searching the scripture for insight regarding the identity and purpose of the church we have seen refreshing things take place. Grace has been adopted as the foundational norm for unity. Members (men, women, and children) are participating in congregational life in ways that allow them to use the gifts God has given them for the building up of the body. It feels like true community; all believers, children included, are recognized as kingdom participants to be included in the life of the church.

A little over five years ago, when concern for the faith development of our children became a priority, East County began seeking a minister to integrate the children of the congregation into the larger faith community. At that time there was no discussion of gender appropriateness. The position was offered to me for a number of reasons. I had been integrally involved in many aspects of our children's ministry. Members of the church had submitted my name citing gifts and abilities they had seen demonstrated in my service to the church, which they believed indicated a calling to ministry. I had also recently completed an M.A. in Ministry. Mark Love, pulpit minister at East County, was instrumental in my decision to further my education in theology. I remember his words: "Doors for women are opening in the church, Shelley. It is important that there be theologically educated women, who are informed about ministry ready to step through them." When I began the program I could see no doors, when I was done one stood wide open

It may seem odd that I did not immediately charge through that door. But my acceptance of the position came after careful consideration. I did not want to be seen as a trailblazer or a troublemaker. While East County had carefully studied the "controversial" Biblical passages and had come to certain conclusions regarding the degree of participation "appropriate" for women in the church, I knew that our understandings were not shared by many in our tradition. News that there was woman employed as a ministerial staff member would get around. Could I, a woman (apart from my inadequacies as an fallible human) really be a leader in the church? Contribute ideas? Exercise judgment? Discern and apply scripture in relation to the Lord's work? Could I do these things without disrespecting my heritage? Did they want to call me something else? Children's Ministry Coordinator perhaps? No. The elders were firm. The desire of the congregation was that I minister to the spiritual needs of our children, "Let's call her what we want her to be, a minister."

And so for the past five years I have ministered within the comfort of the church of my childhood. On occasion I am still caught by the fear that I will offend. When I stand before the congregation to preface a baby dedication with scripture and reflection, or present the call to worship during a Family Worship Sunday, or host a Children's Sunday and happen to catch the eyes of a visitor, I worry that my participation will disrupt their encounter with God in the worship. And so I breathe a quick prayer asking the Spirit to intercede and act on behalf of harmony and peace.

Roles for women are emerging as the church continues to engage in conversation and reflection upon the word of God and the mission of the church to seek and save the lost. As D'Esta Love observes in her transparent article, *Why Am I Afraid?* "Greater avenues of service are opening for women in the church, and we are doing a better job of helping men and women identify their gifts in the Kingdom. We have more women in graduate Bible programs in our Christian colleges, preparing to give their lives to the service of the Lord, and I am confident he will find ways to use them. We live in a time of struggle and change, but I believe it is a time of courage and hope."[xxv]

I take courage and find hope in the power of the Spirit. As we continue to explore what it means to "live in community" and strive to reflect the nature of God, I am confident that we will be led to recognize that the nature of God is reflected in full fellowship. We are the image of God as we share together.

Young and old, rich and poor, male and female. I am hopeful that the differences between the sexes will less and less be seen as reason for exclusion from certain aspects of church participation, but will rather compel us to encourage women and men to serve together in church life. The distinctions between male and female are not reason for prohibition; their expressions create diversity and balance, reflecting the dynamic, relational nature of God, himself. It is exciting to envision the potential for genuine renewal in ministry that could very well be forthcoming as more and more women are encouraged and welcomed to answer ministry callings from our Lord.

-Shelley Neilson, is an early generation Xer who holds a bachelor's degree from Columbia Christian College in counseling education and a master's degree in ministry from Pepperdine University. When Shelly was asked why she was working toward a degree that professionally she would "never use" she replied, "I'll leave that to the Lord." Today the Lord has provided and Shelly is one of a small cadre of women serving congregations as staff members. Her congregation, East County, where she is the children's minister, is committed to the "nurture model" of ministry that stresses the important place of each child in the church now. Her expansive job description includes serving as "vision caster" for the theological orientation guiding the direction of ministry and performing a wide range of varied tasks. In addition to her ministry role, Shelly is an adjunct professor of Bible at Cascade College, Portland, and a frequent speaker at women's events.

Chapter 37
Finality

Part of me is scared and awed by the hidden dimension that will suddenly become my reality. I'd like to stay around for a bit. On the good days, I have a lists of reasons why. On the bad days, not so many. I'm especially anxious about dying a slow death —where I linger while others are burdened with my care.

The "unknown" is the problem. No one can say for sure what we're going to find at the other end of this. It's the best-kept secret around, considering billions of us will discover it one way or another. Categorically, we know that God is at the other end, but am I emotionally ready to find out?

People who know say grief is its own education. I guess you learn things while drowning that you can't learn on solid ground. The rest of us drive by funeral homes and jog through cemeteries every day without thinking too much about it. My wife follows the obituary columns regularly, keeping track of who's still here and who's not. It's a short jaunt between those two points. A woman who survived a shooting rampage said she realized that she was much more fragile than she ever thought she was. The only thing that keeps any of us here is the tiny rush of air that makes our chests rise and fall. When that involuntary action ceases, we float away. My mother died on the last day of December, 1994. I miss her. I didn't get to say all that I needed to say to her. That's scary, and it's lousy, but it's true.

Yesterday, I visited my 76-year-old father-in-law. He gazed at me as if to say his life was on the downhill curve and mine was on the uphill curve. It dawned on me that he might not even be around next month, but that's not something we openly discussed. Sometimes I wonder what it is that we are trying to keep hidden from each other? As Timothy Leary puts it, "First, everybody knows you're dying. So what do they do? They come over and talk about Aunt Millie's new car and who won the

World Cup. Like you're suddenly an idiot and need to be diverted."

Talk about death, and you'll get mixed reactions. Some faces will go completely blank. Others will wince. Some think it's morbid, and others are fascinated. But the truth is no one likes to talk about death. Not many of us even like to think about it. But it's the one certain thing in life. It's coming. As Rebecca Faber points out, "One hundred out of one hundred people die. One hundred percent. Knowing that helps, I guess, because if it happens to everyone, you are not being persecuted. Death is no respecter of persons. It's universal, and we are not being singled out for some solitary punishment. Ahead of everyone on the face of the earth, sometime, is death. Sooner or later."[xxvi]

Conclusion

Henry Peterson was a high school football star, recruited to play for Brown University, but at Brown, Peterson became a benchwarmer. In Peterson's senior year, the week before the big game with Yale, tragedy struck; Peterson's father died. Now he had a dilemma; should he abandon the team before the big game to be with his family or should he stay? The coach made it easy for him; he told Peterson that his family needed him more than they did and that the team would say a prayer for him on game day.

Game day comes and who walks into the locker room, dressed, and ready to play, but benchwarmer Henry Peterson! The coach goes up to him and says, "I told you to go home. What are you doing here?"

Peterson responded, "I know, Coach, but I had to be here, and I've got a favor to ask."

The Coach says, "Anything, son."

"I need to start the game today."

The Coach had a soft side; he told Peterson that he could start, but the minute he screwed up, he would be back on the bench.

Peterson took the field, rushed for over 100 yards, scored two touchdowns and Brown won the game. The Coach went up to Peterson after the game, half furious, and said, "You sat on my bench for four years. Why didn't you let me know you could play like that? Peterson responded, "Coach, did you ever meet my dad?"

"No, son, I never had the pleasure."

"Did you ever see us walking arm-in-arm along the campus?"

"No son, what's your point?"

"Coach, my dad was blind, and today was the first day he could see me play."

Henry Peterson taught us an important lesson that day. Bench warming is a choice. Will you sit on life's sidelines, or will you take the ball and run with it? Will you affect real and meaningful change within your home congregation so that a new generation might come to know Jesus?

In closing, poet Ralph Waldo Emerson has a great job description for a change agent:

> To laugh often and much;
> To appreciate beauty;
> To find the best in others;
> To leave the world a bit better,
> whether by a healthy child,
> a garden patch,
> or a redeemed social condition
> To know even one life has breathed easier because you have lived;
> That is to have succeeded.

Epilogue

We live in a wild universe, a universe in which the absolute truth is frightening. Go outside at night in the country, where the sky is very clear. Then look up. Each one of those tiny points in the sky is a flaming sun. We're a tiny part of an enormous universe which may be one of many universes. No one really knows for sure what's out there. So we use our imagination. Imagination allows us to ask big questions, questions that scare us and for which we don't have easy answers.

Human beings are born with a great deal of creativity and imagination, but by the age of twelve, we've lost most of it. The world just slams it out of us. Our teachers and parents tell us that what comes from our imagination isn't true; it's just "imaginary." Creativity comes from accepting that you're not safe, from letting go of control. It's a matter of seeing everything—even when you want to shut your eyes.

In a world of constant change, innovation, and creativity will be the difference between churches that grow and churches that become relics of the past. Church leaders who relinquish control and allow their followships the freedom to explore their creativity will fluidly navigate this postmodern era. Real creativity is life altering; it threatens the status quo; it makes us see things differently, and it brings about change. Change always threatens our comfort, but we must change!

Chapter 1

[i] Knight, G. *The Pharisee's Guide to Perfect Holiness*. Pacific Press Publishing, Boise, ID, 1992, P. 16.

[ii] Paden, R. From the Churches of Christ to the Bostom Movement: A Comparative Study. Masters Thesis, University of Kansas, 1994.

[iii] Campbell, A. "Any Christians Among the Sects?" *Millennial Harbinger*, 564-565, 1837.

[iv] Stone, B. "Desultory Remarks," *Christian Messenger*, 182, 1836 (December).

[v] Squire, R. Where is the Bible Silent: Essays on the Campbell-Stone Religious Restoration of America, Southland Press, Los Angeles, CA, 1973, P. 23.

[vi] Etter, C. "In Search of Freedom," *Voices of Concern*, 1966, P. 107.

[vii] Weed, M. (Professor of Theology and Ethics at the Institute for Christian Studies) "A Tradition at Risk," *Christian Studies*, 1991 (Spring), P. 52.

[viii] Paden, R. From the Churches of Christ to the Boston Movement: A Comparative Study. Master Thesis, University of Kansas, 1994.

Chapter 2

[ix] The majority of the Pharisees rules were handed down through oral tradition. Pharisaic tradition held to the belief that "Moses received the Law from Sinai and committed it to Joshua, and Joshua committed it to the elders, and the elders to the Prophets, and the Prophets committed it to the leaders of the Synagogue. They said three things: Be deliberate in judgment, raise up many disciples, and make a fence around the Law (m. Aboth 1:1)

[x] Corban is a technical term meaning "a gift or offering."

Chapter 3

[xi] of or relating to Arius or his doctrines especially that the Son is not of the same substance as the Father but was created as an agent for creating the world.

Chapter 9

I am indebted to Dennis McCallum for much of the material in this chapter.

Chapter 11

[xii] Genesis 5:29

[xiii] From "The Message" Eugene Peterson. John 2:1-11

[xiv] Someone has calculated this to measure to nine hundred fifths of wine. At an average cost of thirty dollars a bottle, Jesus produced twenty-seven thousand dollars' worth of wine that day.

Chapter 13

[xv] The Greek word *katagraphein* literally means to "write down" and connotes a process of listing.

Chapter 18

[xvi] Church of Christ tradition and scholarship would consider Isaiah 11:6-9 to be a figurative passage. Yet, we must not limit our God who is capable of bringing about the described conditions in a literal fashion.

Chapter 20

[xvii] Nouwen, was born and ordained a priest in the Netherlands and trained as a psychologist in Kansas. Nouwen wrote more than 40 books. He taught at Notre Dame, Harvard, and Yale universities and spent the last 10 years of his life at L'Arche Daybreak, a community

in the Toronto suburbs where disabled and able-bodied people live together. He died suddenly of a heart attack in 1996 at the age of 64.

Chapter 29

[xviii] Marcus Barth was a Professor at the Pittsburgh Theological Seminary, 1973-85

[xix] Jubilee 1999 session in Nashville

[xx] Jean Vanier is Canadian, born in 1928, son of the late Governor General of Canada. Educated in England and Canada; for several years, he was with the British Navy then with the Canadian Royal Navy. In 1950, he resigned from the Navy, went to France and worked on a doctorate in Philosophy (on Aristotle) which he received from the "Institut Catholique de Paris,". In 1964, with Raphaël Simi and Philippe Seux, two men with developmental disabilities, he founded L'Arche, a community with men and women who have developmental disabilities, many coming from psychiatric centers. From this original community in France, one hundred and three communities were founded throughout the world, in Europe, Africa, Asia, North and South America. In 1968, in Merylake, Ontario, a community called "Faith and Sharing" was founded following a retreat preached by Jean Vanier, a community where people gather at least once a month to share the Gospel.

[xxi] Jim Wallis is an author, a preacher, a pastor, and an activist. He is also co-founder of the Sojourners Community in inner-city Washington, D.C., as well as editor-in-chief of *Sojourners* magazine, a bimonthly publication examining issues of faith, politics, and culture.

Chapter 34

[xxii] Not everything is subject to change. Scripture must never be changed but our methods of teaching and reaching the lost of our era must be as fluid as our culture.

[xxiii] Neo-traditions are traditions customized and personalized.

Chapter 36

[xxiv] These are the words of Mark Love, Minister of the Word for ten years at the East County Church of Christ in Gresham, Oregon. Love has facilitated the development of a discernment model for ministry that says that God is doing something by calling particular people together and it is up to them to figure that out.

[xxv] D Esta Love.° Why Am I Afraid? ° LEAVEN (Spring, 1996) 4-6.

Chapter 37

[xxvi] Ms. Faber graduated from the University of Victoria in 1993 and was called to the bar in May, 1994. In addition to an LL.B., she holds an Associate of Arts in Business Administration (1987) and a Bachelor of Arts (1990). Ms. Faber has received awards for excellence in business administration, marketing, and wills drafting. Ms. Faber practices in the areas of wills and estates, personal injury litigation and family law. She sits on occasion as a moot court judge at the University of Victoria Law School and lectures regularly on family law topics. Prior to entering the legal profession, Ms. Faber worked as an editor and as an insurance broker.

www.ingramcontent.com/pod-product-compliance
Lightning Source LLC
Chambersburg PA
CBHW031358040426
42444CB00005B/338